These Are The Times That Try Women's Souls

A Bible Study that addresses the question,
*"Has anyone ever lived **my life** and survived with*
faith intact?"

Lessons Prepared by
Emily Andrews Kile

Cover Photos
by
Mali Voloshin-Kile

ISBN: 0-89137-471-X

Introduction

Perhaps your first response to this question is, "But you don't understand. My circumstances are unique." You might go on to explain your response with true statements such as:

"I live in an area of the country where the church is weak."

"The schools my children attend are run by gangs."

"My husband's job requires us to move every few years, and that's hard on the family."

"I'm a single mother and must work in order to keep food on the table."

"When I married, I expected my husband to be spiritually supportive of my efforts to serve the Lord. Things didn't turn out that way."

"I became involved in sinful lifestyles before I came to know the Lord, and now it is impossible for me to extricate myself."

"I just don't have the ability to stand before the world and proclaim the truth."

And the list goes on.

In a sense we all live in unique circumstances. These "times" that try our souls are surely the worst ever—at least from our perspective. As children created by God, we possess qualities that no one else shares completely. But as we look back at the women who lived during Old Testament times and see the circumstances they faced, the sense of being unique is overshadowed by the realization of another great truth: "We are one." The very uniqueness of God's creation called "Woman" brings us together. If we look carefully, we will see ourselves and our circumstances mirrored in God's word. The daughters, sisters, wives, mothers, grandmothers, career women, queens, princesses, slaves, and prostitutes, whose life stories are interwoven throughout the history of God's people, faced the same decisions, dealt with the same problems, reacted with the same passion (or lack of passion), and overcame the same obstacles that we face today. Some were successful; some failed miserably. All were part of God's perfect plan.

As we study the lives of these women, perhaps we can draw strength from them, and gain insights that will help us overcome the difficulties we face daily. God has promised us that such a study will give us hope.

Romans 15:4 For everything that was written in the past, was written to teach us, so that through endurance and the encouragement of the scripture, we might have hope.

3

These Are The Times That Try Women's Souls

Has Anyone Experienced My Life and Survived with Faith Intact?

Although we are familiar with many women in the Bible, it is not always easy to picture them as ordinary people who lived lives that were in various respects similar to ours. We may look at Sarah and see her in special circumstances that set her apart from us. After all, her husband was Abraham, the father of the faithful. Or perhaps we think of Deborah, the Judge, leading the Israelite army, something we will surely never be called upon to do. How can we possibly relate to her? Will we be challenged as Esther was, and need the courage to say, "...If I perish, I perish?"

Looking more closely at these women and the times in which they lived, it becomes easier to recognize the similarities in our lives. Each era of Jewish history had unique problems that women had to face. All of these women could have said with us, "These are the times that try women's souls."

Patriarchal Times

The women who lived during this time period participated in the beginning of the nation that would eventually bring Christ into the world. This was a special privilege, and should have given meaning to anyone's life, however mundane. But when we consider the fact that these women had no written word to give them access to the mind of God, their task appears more difficult. Many times years would pass during which they had no specific communication with God as to what constituted their role in his plan . Mostly their lives consisted of the daily grind: meal preparation, child care, laundry, etc., all of which had to be accomplished with very few amenities and probably little recognition or thanks.

As we look at the lives of Sarah and Hagar we see many of the situations that face us today: The desire for a child; The conflict between brothers; A divided family; A young man deprived of a father. Perhaps one or more of these problems has a familiar ring to your ears. How did these women deal with these obstacles? Will their experiences help us?

From Egyptian Bondage to The Establishment of a Kingdom

This period of Israel's history may have been the most difficult. Many women were born and spent their lives as slaves, often feeling the lash of the taskmaster's whip. Others wandered for years in the wilderness, not knowing from one day to the next where they would spend the following night. For some, God's love and protection was evident, often taken for granted, and eventually lost. Then survival became the only motive for life. Even in such circumstances, these women had the normal responsibilities of everyday life. All faced the harsh realities of sickness, sin, and death. Although their lives would later be used to teach a lost world about the blessings of Christ, to them life must have often seemed pointless.

Women such as Miriam and Deborah held positions of responsibility and were constantly in the public eye. You may face the problems that such a life produces. Jochebed's primary function was that of a mother. How did she handle all the difficulties that are part of that job description? Rahab and Delilah both were prostitutes, but their lives took very different turns. How can we benefit from their experiences?

The United Kingdoms

We see women living very different lives during Israel's time as a world power. The scriptures give us intimate portraits of those who were daughters of kings, mothers of kings, and wives of kings. Their circumstances are unique—we are not likely to qualify in any of these categories—but the problems they faced are strikingly like our own. We have to look a little more closely to find the "ordinary" woman of these times, but she is there as well, challenging us with her determination and perseverance.

Michal and Abigail were both married to David, but that is about all they have in common. Each came into David's life under unique circumstances. The attitude displayed by each was a determining factor in the outcome of their lives. Jeroboam's wife is perhaps a small footnote in the history of Israel, but she, too, has an important lesson to teach us.

From the Divided Kingdom Through the Exile

As the Old Testament draws to a close, God's plan of salvation begins to come into sharper focus. The women who are active in support of truth often suffer the ultimate consequence and surrender their lives to the service of God. Others who oppose God bring him ultimate glory by their own destruction. The women who saw their chosen nation finally brought to its knees and carried away into exile must have found it difficult to hold on to any shred of hope. How did these "mothers in exile" manage to face each day in a godless society and still teach their children that "there is a better way?" How could they hope to combat such overwhelming pressures? A study of their lives serves to give us hope.

Queen Esther certainly captures our imagination. As a member of a Jewish family that had chosen to remain in exile, she became the wife of the most powerful monarch in the world at the time. How can we relate to her? What part did she play in God's plan for my salvation?

Here are some questions we might ask ourselves as we look at the lives of these women:

- Were they actively supportive of God's plan?
- Were they actively opposed to God's plan?
- What was it in their lives that made it possible for God to use them?
- How can we benefit from their lives?

What Can We Expect From Our Times?

God does not leave us in the dark concerning what we can expect from the world around us. Jesus told his disciples plainly what they could expect as a result of following him.

> *John 15:19 If you belonged to the world, it would love you as its own. As it is, you do not belong to the world, but I have chosen you out of the world. That is why the world hates you.*

John 16:33a "I have told you these things, so that in me you may have peace. In this world you will have trouble..."

2 Tim 3:2 People will be lovers of themselves, lovers of money, boastful, proud, abusive, disobedient to their parents, ungrateful, unholy, without love, unforgiving, slanderous, without self-control, brutal, not lovers of the good, treacherous, rash, conceited, lovers of pleasure rather than lovers of God— having a form of godliness but denying its power. Have nothing to do with them.

2 Tim 4:3 For the time will come when men will not put up with sound doctrine. Instead, to suit their own desires, they will gather around them a great number of teachers to say what their itching ears want to hear.

There is no doubt about the fulfillment of these prophecies. We should not be surprised when we see the condition of the world around us. The trying times in which we live are very accurately described in the scriptures.

What Should Be Our Response to These Trying Times?

God did not leave us with this horrifying picture of the world without giving us some instructions on how to survive. Being aware of the situation gives us the opportunity to prepare ourselves. We have a responsibility to those around us.

Mat 5:13-14 "You are the salt of the earth. But if the salt loses its saltiness, how can it be made salty again? It is no longer good for anything, except to be thrown out and trampled by men. You are the light of the world. A city on a hill cannot be hidden.

Mat 6:25 "Therefore I tell you, do not worry about your life, what you will eat or drink; or about your body, what you will wear. Is not life more important than food, and the body more important than clothes?

Rom 12:1-2 Therefore, I urge you, brothers, in view of God's mercy, to offer your bodies as living sacrifices, holy and pleasing to God—this is your spiritual act of worship. Do not conform any longer to the pattern of this world, but be transformed by the renewing of your mind. Then you will be able to test and approve what God's will is—his good, pleasing and perfect will.

Eph 5:15-16 Be very careful, then, how you live—not as unwise but as wise, making the most of every opportunity, because the days are evil.

Col 3:2 Set your minds on things above, not on earthly things.

Titus 2:12-14 It teaches us to say "No" to ungodliness and worldly passions, and to live self-controlled, upright and godly lives in this present age, while we wait for the blessed hope— the glorious appearing of our great God and Savior, Jesus Christ, who gave himself for us to redeem us from all wickedness and to purify for himself a people that are his very own, eager to do what is good.

1 Pet 1:14 As obedient children, do not conform to the evil desires you had when you lived in ignorance.

1 Pet 2:11 Dear friends, I urge you, as aliens and strangers in the world, to abstain from sinful desires, which war against your soul.

1 John 2:15-17 Do not love the world or anything in the world. If anyone loves the world, the love of the Father is not in him. For everything in the world—the cravings of sinful man, the lust of his eyes and the boasting of what he has and does—comes not from the Father but from the world. The world and its desires pass away, but the man who does the will of God lives forever.

What Is the Reward for Responding Correctly To Our Times?

Jn 16:33b "...But take heart! I have overcome the world."

Rom 8:18 I consider that our present sufferings are not worth comparing with the glory that will be revealed in us.

2 Cor 4:16-18 Therefore we do not lose heart. Though outwardly we are wasting away, yet inwardly we are being renewed day by day. For our light and momentary troubles are achieving for us an eternal glory that far outweighs them all. So we fix our eyes not on what is seen, but on what is unseen. For what is seen is temporary, but what is unseen is eternal.

Phil 2:15-16 so that you may become blameless and pure, children of God without fault in a crooked and depraved generation, in which you shine like stars in the universe as you hold out the word of life—in order that I may boast on the day of Christ that I did not run or labor for nothing.

Who are God's Women of the 20th and 21st century?

Every woman who lives in these trying times fits somewhere in God's plan. All have the potential to qualify as women of God. What does it take? Can we possibly hope to meet the requirements? Does God need us at all today? After all, the plan of salvation is already in place; Christ has already made the ultimate sacrifice that gives us eternal life. What is left for us to do? The answer, of course, is "Spread the word." Whatever situation we find ourselves in provides a unique opportunity for sharing Christ. We **can** be women of God.

Patriarchal	Slavery/Exodus	Conquest/Judge	Kingdoms	Exile
2100-1900 B.C.	1800-1500 B.C.	1400-1100 B.C.	1000-600 B.C.	600-500 B.C.
Sarah	Jochebed	Rahab	Michal	Vashti
Lot's Wife	Miriam	Debora	Abigail	Esther
Hagar	Pharaoh's Daughter	Samson's Mother	Bathsheba	Mother in Exile
Rebekah	Zipporah	Delilah	Tamar	
Leah		Naomi	Queen of Sheba	
Rachel		Ruth	Jeroboam's Wife	
Dinah		Orpah	Widow of Zarephath	
Tamar		Hannah	Jezebel	
Asenath			Shunamite Woman	
Potiphars's Wife			Athaliah	
			Huldah	

Find scripture references for each of these women. Add names of other women who lived during these periods of history.

Sarah, Princess

I was born to Terah around the year 2156 B.C.

I married my half-brother, Abram, who was ten years older than I.

I lived in Ur of the Chaldeans until God called my husband to an unknown land.

I moved with Abram, my father Terah, my nephew Lot, and other family members to Haran where I lived until age 65.

After my father died, I journeyed with Abram to the land of Canaan.

Although my husband's name meant "exalted father," I was barren.

Because I was unable to have a child, I gave my maid to my husband, that I might have a child through her.

God spoke to my husband when I was 89 and told him that I would bear a child.

By faith, at age 90, I gave birth to my only son, Isaac.

When my son was weaned, the son of my maid mocked him. With God's approval they were sent away.

I died at age 127, and was buried by husband in the land of Canaan.

And let not your adornment be merely external--braiding the hair, and wearing gold jewelry, or putting on dresses; but let it be the hidden person of the heart, with the imperishable quality of a gentle and quiet spirit, which is precious in the sight of God. For in this way in former times the holy women also, who hoped in God, used to adorn themselves, being submissive to their own husbands. Thus Sarah obeyed Abraham, calling him lord, and you have become her children if you do what is right without being frightened by any fear.
1 Peter 3:3-6

Has Life Passed Me By?
Sarah, the Princess
Genesis 12-23

If someone had asked you ten years ago where you would be and what you would be doing at this point in your life, how would your answer compare with the reality of today? Suppose they had asked you five years ago? or even six months ago? The woman of God who we will study in this lesson probably never dreamed what her life would be like in her "golden years."

Just the Facts

Born about 400 years after the flood and 2,000 years before Christ, Sarah is first mentioned in *Genesis 11:29-30* as she approached the age of sixty-five. She is most often identified as Abraham's wife, and was ten years younger than he. When we meet her she was known by the name of Sarai, and was already considered a barren woman.

Sarah's life is divided almost exactly in half. The first part was spent in Ur of the Chaldeans, a highly civilized city that was steeped in idolatry. Recently archaeologists have uncovered parts of the city, giving us insight into everyday life. Libraries contain dictionaries, encyclopedias, and other books, as well as records of property disputes, the administration of justice, canal building, money-lending, and worship of the gods. From these findings we can assume that Sarah lived in a house and enjoyed the many "modern conveniences" provided by civilization. She certainly lived there long enough to grow accustomed to such things.

When Abram was called by God to leave Ur, Sarah accompanied him to Haran where they lived until she was sixty-five years old. From Haran she followed her husband to Canaan, without knowing why. Though already into middle age, Sarah willingly left a well-developed culture, friends and family, and an established dwelling, to go to an unknown land, an uncertain future, and a nomadic lifestyle. This would be comparable to the "culture shock" we might experience by leaving the United States to live in Haiti. Sarah accepted her husband's role in God's plan, even if she did not understand it.

As we look at Sarah's life in Canaan ten years later, we find that she was still barren. At the age of seventy-five, knowing that God had promised Abraham descendants, she gave her maidservant to him, intending to accept any child that might come from Hagar as her own. Ishmael was born from this union, but things did not turn out as Sarah expected. Another fifteen years passed before, at the age of ninety, she gave birth to her only child, Isaac.

The events surrounding the birth of Isaac make up the major part of Sarah's life that is revealed to us. Many years pass with no description of her daily activities. What must it have been like? Abraham was wealthy and respected, but owned no real estate. Sarah probably had a nice, fancy tent, but it was still a tent. She may have wondered often, "Why are we here?"

After Isaac was weaned, we hear no more of Sarah until her death thirty-four years later. She must have spent much of this time with Isaac and formed close bonds with her only son. Isaac's personality seems to be evidence of this. He was a quiet, peace-loving man, preferring to spend most of his time "at home."

Sarah is the only woman in the Bible whose age is given at her death. She was 127 years old. Abraham buried her in the cave of Macpelah which he had bought for that purpose.

> *Gen 23:1-2 Sarah lived to be a hundred and twenty-seven years old. She died at Kiriath Arba (that is, Hebron) in the land of Canaan, and Abraham went to mourn for Sarah and to weep over her.*

Three years after his mother's death Isaac still mourned her loss. He brought his wife Rebekah to Sarah's tent and was finally comforted. *Gen 24:67*

Sarah's Fear: Has Life Passed Me By?

Sarah is often criticized for her behavior at certain times in her life. When we look at the incident involving Hagar, it is easy for us to point out Sarah's **lack of faith** and her **unwillingness to wait on God**. Perhaps we fail to realize that she was not specifically named in the promise that Abraham's seed would be multiplied. After God had told Abraham that he would have a child of his own *(Gen 15:4)*, fourteen years passed with apparently no word from God, and Sarah was still barren. She sought to advance God's will by using her own wisdom: giving Hagar to Abraham. This was an acceptable practice in the culture of the time.

> *"If she has given a maid to her husband and she has borne children and afterwards that maid has made herself equal with her mistress, because she has borne children her mistress shall not sell her for money, she shall reduce her to bondage and count her among the female slaves." From the Laws of King Hammurabi*

14

Although her motives seemed to be good, Sarah did not antici-
pate her own reaction, nor that of Hagar. We will deal more fully
with this incident in our next lesson when we look specifically at
Hagar.

Sarah, convinced that life had indeed passed her by, reacted with
doubt when first hearing that she would bear a child.

> *Gen 18:12 So Sarah laughed to herself as she thought, "After
> I am worn out and my master is old, will I now have this
> pleasure?"*

Who wouldn't have laughed? It had been fourteen years since
the birth of Ishmael. Sarah was now eighty-nine years old. This
pronouncement came from one whom she recognized as God's
messenger. Apparently she felt she knew herself and her capabilities
better than God did. Sarah is in good company here; the scriptures tell of
many others who have had the same feelings: Moses, Gideon, Jeremiah.
Her faith grew as God's plan unfolded. Indeed she did conceive, and
rejoiced in that fact. The name "Isaac" reflected both her doubt and her
joyous faith.

Sarah's Strong Points

The characteristics of Sarah's life that are held up as examples
for us to follow far outweigh the weaknesses that occasionally
appear.

> *1 Pet 3:3-5 Your beauty should not come from outward adorn-
> ment, such as braided hair and the wearing of gold jewelry
> and fine clothes. Instead, it should be that of your inner self,
> the unfading beauty of a gentle and quiet spirit, which is of
> great worth in God's sight. For this is the way the holy women
> of the past who put their hope in God used to make them-
> selves beautiful. They were submissive to their own husbands,
> like Sarah, who obeyed Abraham and called him her master.
> You are her daughters if you do what is right and do not give
> way to fear.*

First of all, we are told that Sarah had **Inner Beauty.** She was
chaste and respectful, having adorned the inside of herself as well as
the outer. She had a gentle and quiet spirit and hoped in God. No
matter what our limitations, we can all cultivate a gentle and quiet
spirit, which is of great worth in God's sight.

15

The next characteristic we notice is **Submission**. Sarah's role as a submissive wife grows with our understanding of the uncertain life she lived. She submitted in the initial move from Ur. She submitted to Abraham when Lot apparently took the best part of the land. She even submitted when Abraham lied about their relationship, although it put her in danger. She did not allow her own doubts and fears to overcome her. Had she done so, Abraham's life would have been one of misery.

Another characteristic that Sarah had was **Faith**.

> *Heb 11:11 By faith even Sarah herself received ability to conceive, even beyond the proper time of life, since she considered Him faithful who had promised...*

At one point in her life, Sarah suffered because of her lack of faith, but her faith grew as God's plan unfolded. Each step she took in faith taught her that God was faithful to keep His promises. Evidently her faith had a part in Isaac's birth, the single most important event in her life.

Sarah's Greatest Challenges

We all face challenges in our lives. We are able to routinely deal with and dispose of some, but others take considerably more effort, and may persist throughout our lifetimes. Sarah faced many challenges in her life. Most of them were no different than the ones we face in these trying times.

One challenge Sarah faced was being the **wife of one such as Abraham**. You remember Abraham: the father of the faithful, the friend of God, the beginning of the Jewish nation, righteous Abraham, etc.? What a privilege to be married to such a man! What a challenge! God has a standard for those women who would be wives to His leaders.

> *1 Tim 3:11 In the same way, their wives are to be women worthy of respect, not malicious talkers but temperate and trustworthy in everything.*

Another challenge that Sarah faced is familiar to many women in the world today. While Sarah's husband's name meant "exalted father", Sarah was **barren** even before they left Ur. Being a barren woman in a society that considered it a disgrace, even a curse, must have caused her great anguish. She may have felt that she was hindering

Abraham from being what God wanted him to be. There is perhaps no greater challenge than to feel you are the reason for someone else's spiritual failure. Realizing that God is faithful to fulfill His promises will help us to keep our perspective.

Sarah did eventually bear a child, but her value to us is based on something entirely different. Her quiet, gentle spirit was of great value to God, and Paul's letter to the Galatian Christians says that her "spiritual" children share a greater blessing through faith in Christ than her physical children obtained by virtue of birth. *(Galatians 4:27)*

Sarah and Abraham never really had a **permanent home** after leaving Ur. They were always on the move. Many of you have faced this challenge and understand the difficulties that come as a result. It seems hardly worth the effort to make friends when separation is only a matter of time. The children just get settled in a new school when, for one reason or another, it's time to move again. It was necessary for Abraham and Sarah to move in order to be separated from an idolatrous world. In spite of the hardships that resulted, they accepted the challenge. We are similarly challenged.

> *2 Cor 6:17-18 "Therefore come out from them and be separate, says the Lord. Touch no unclean thing, and I will receive you. I will be a Father to you, and you will be my sons and daughters, says the Lord Almighty."*

While never having a permanent home can be a challenge, it can also serve as a constant reminder to us that our citizenship is firmly fixed in another land that bears the imprint of permanence. Our ties to the family of God serve to overcome the insecurities and discouragement that arise from the mobile lifestyle many of us are forced to live.

Sarah faced another challenge that we might see as a great asset: her **outward beauty.** When we look more closely, we can see that it truly was a great challenge. It caused her husband anxiety and twice led him to sin:

> *Gen 12:12-13 When the Egyptians see you, they will say, 'This is his wife.' Then they will kill me but will let you live. Say you are my sister, so that I will be treated well for your sake and my life will be spared because of you."*

It even endangered Sarah's place in God's plan.

> *Gen 20:6 Then God said to him in the dream, "Yes, I know you did this with a clear conscience, and so I have kept you*

from sinning against me. That is why I did not let you touch her..."

Abimelech, the Philistine leader involved in this incident, must have been planning to "touch" her. This incident took place shortly before the birth of Isaac. Had God not intervened, it could have cast doubt on Isaac's parentage. The problems caused by outward beauty can be numerous. Perhaps this is why God directed Peter to caution women of God to pay more attention to our inner beauty.

Overcoming **feelings of inadequacy** in the face of Hagar's contempt was a challenge that Sarah was unable to overcome. Her outward beauty did not help her when her maid servant had conceived a child by Abraham. Her exalted position as number one wife to a wealthy prince did not help her. It took many years of pain and despair for Sarah to find her sense of adequacy in the promises of the Lord. After denying that she had the ability to accomplish what God had planned for her, she was finally able to accept her role by faith. Long after even the faintest hope of bearing Abraham's child had passed, Isaac was born, and Sarah was able to rejoice and share her joy with all who would hear her story.

Conclusion

Perhaps the most surprising thing about Sarah's life is the realization that her greatest work for the Lord was done when she felt that life had passed her by. She spent the last thirty-seven years of her life, after she was ninety years old, raising a child. More than likely we will not be asked to raise a child at that advanced age. However, our most important work may be done in later life. We must keep our options open.

> *Eccl 11:6 Sow your seed in the morning, and at evening let not your hands be idle, for you do not know which will succeed, whether this or that, or whether both will do equally well.*

Sarah had a special role to fulfill in God's plan of salvation. Christ would come into the world through the nation that began with Abraham and Sarah. The difficult situation created because of her desire for a child serves as an allegory that shows the superiority of the law of faith over the law of Moses.

> *Gal 4:24 These things may be taken figuratively, for the women represent two covenants. One covenant is from Mount*

Sinai and bears children who are to be slaves: This is Hagar...
Now you, brothers, like Isaac, are children of promise.

Surely Sarah would have classified her "times" as trying to a woman's soul. Although her role in God's plan was unique, she left an example for all of us to follow.

Sarai - My Princess
Sarah - Princess of Multitudes

STRONG POINTS	GREATEST CHALLENGES

I can benefit most from Sarah's life in the following ways:

Hagar, the Egyptian

I lived in Egypt until Pharaoh gave me to Abraham as a gift.

For ten years I served as Sarah's personal maid.

Because Sarah was barren, she gave me to Abraham as a secondary wife, intending to accept my child as her own.

I became proud and arrogant because I had conceived and Sarah could not.

Sarah mistreated me (with Abraham's permission), and I fled into the desert to escape.

The angel of the Lord found me there and sent me back to submit to Sarah.

I gave birth to a son and Abraham named him Ishmael.

Although Sarah did not accept him. Ishmael was loved by Abraham and treated as his heir.

Fourteen years after Ishmael's birth, Sarah herself gave birth to Isaac.

Because Ishmael mocked Isaac, Sarah demanded that Abraham send us away.

With God's approval, Abraham did so, even though it was painful for him.

As God promised, my son grew to manhood in the desert and became the father of 12 sons. Their descendants are antagonistic toward Isaac's descendants even to this day.

More than 2,000 years after my death, the apostle Paul used the events in my life to contrast the law of sin and death with the law of promise that came through Isaac's seed: Christ.

...You brethren, like Isaac, are children of promise. But as at that time he who was born according to the flesh persecuted him who was born according to the Spirit, so it is now also. But what does the scripture say: Cast out the bondwoman and her son, for the son of the bondwoman shall not be an heir with the son of the free woman. So then, brethren, we are not children of a bondwoman, but of the free woman.
Galatians 4:24-31

Can God Use the Fruit of a Broken Home?
Hagar, the Egyptian
Genesis 16, 21

Just a piece of property. That's what Hagar was. Perhaps she considered herself fortunate to belong to Abraham, since his slaves were treated more humanely than many others. And to be personal maid to Sarah was definitely an enviable position. But the life of a slave is never certain. Things changed for Hagar. At first the change seemed to be a positive one: She was chosen to bear the master's child. It soon became apparent, however, that she was just being used, and abuse, as is often the case, followed. That was only the beginning of Hagar's emotional roller coaster ride.

Just the Facts

Hagar was an Egyptian slave who belonged to Sarah. She was most likely acquired during a visit made to Egypt early in Abraham's sojourn in Canaan. This was one of the occasions when he asked Sarah to say she was his sister instead of his wife. Pharaoh's desire for Sarah caused him to shower gifts on Abraham. Following Pharaoh's discovery that he had been deceived, he sent them back to Canaan with all their possessions. Hagar was probably one of the servants in this transaction.

> *Gen 12:16 He treated Abram well for her sake, and Abram acquired sheep and cattle, male and female donkeys, menservants and maidservants, and camels.*

When we are personally introduced to Hagar in the scriptures, she has been with Abraham and Sarah for a decade. Her involvement in the lives of this chosen family will continue through another twenty years. During this time she will play a significant role in the development of God's plan of redemption. Hagar was drawn into the action through no desire of her own. After her forced separation from Abraham's household, she went to live in the desert with her son Ishmael. We hear no more about her until she is mentioned in the New Testament, used there as an example to help us better understand the law of Christ.

The Ride Begins

It didn't take much emotional involvement to be a slave. It was like riding on a roller coaster that went round and round, but stayed on level ground. There were not many decisions to be made. Once your duties were explained, you carried them out as efficiently as possible. But once in a while, an unusual situation would arise. It happened to Hagar, and suddenly her roller coaster began to inch upward. Soon it was soaring toward an unfamiliar high point!

Sarah had chosen her to bear a child to Abraham in an effort to expedite God's promise that he would be the father of nations. This was common practice at the time. According to the Laws of King Hammurabi, a child born in this manner would be the legal heir and could not be displaced by children born later to the actual wife. Of course, Sarah planned for any child that came from the union of Abraham and Hagar to be hers. Still, if Hagar did conceive, surely her status in the household would be elevated.

Perhaps Hagar failed to take into consideration the fact that she was just being used. In such a situation, a person never gains status, but loses it. Apparently, it did not take long until Hagar was convinced that she carried Abraham's child. She may not have realized it, but she was poised at the very top of an emotional ride that would dominate her feelings for years to come.

Life at the Top

Life at the top of the roller coaster lasts for only the briefest measure of time. If you are able to catch your breath, you are lucky. Things were no different for Hagar. The thrill of pregnancy was followed by a feeling of **pride** that led her to exhibit a **disrespectful attitude** toward her mistress. This was followed immediately by the realization that Sarah's attitude toward her had changed.

> *Gen 16:4 He slept with Hagar, and she conceived. When she knew she was pregnant, she began to despise her mistress.*

> *Prov 30:21 "Under three things the earth trembles, under four it cannot bear up: a servant who becomes king, a fool who is full of food, an unloved woman who is married, and a maidservant who displaces her mistress."*

The thrill of knowing that a new life was growing within Hagar may have brought her to an emotional high. Perhaps she thought she could displace Sarah as Abraham's number one wife. At the very least, she would be the mother of his heir. She failed to realize that none of what was happening to her was a result of her own actions, nor did it change who she was: Sarah's servant. We must guard our attitudes when we have the privilege of bearing children. It is a great blessing from God, and should cause us to be humbled by the responsibility entrusted to us.

Hagar's haughty attitude contributed to her own suffering. Not surprisingly, Sarah reacted with **bitterness**. Her inability to conceive had caused her to suffer for more than half a lifetime. This despair erupted into bitterness when Hagar became pregnant with Abraham's child. confirming that Sarah alone was the cause of their childlessness. Sarah, a woman characterized by God as having a meek and quiet spirit, not only lashes out with **recriminations** toward Abraham but **harshness** toward Hagar.

On the Downside

Hagar was allowed little time to enjoy being at the top of the roller coaster. She was made painfully aware of her slavery and subjection. Abraham as much as turned his back on her and their child when he gave Sarah permission to treat Hagar as she saw fit.

> *Gen 16:6 "Your servant is in your hands," Abram said. "Do with her whatever you think best." Then Sarai mistreated Hagar; so she fled from her.*

Pregnant, unmarried, and at the mercy of a mistress to whom she had shown open disrespect, her life seemed to be rushing toward the lowest point imaginable. After ten years of being part of a prosperous household, Hagar fled alone into the desert. She had no one to turn to and nowhere to go.

> *Gen 16:7-9 The angel of the LORD found Hagar near a spring in the desert; it was the spring that is beside the road to Shur. And he said, "Hagar, servant of Sarai, where have you come from, and where are you going?"*
> *"I'm running away from my mistress Sarai," she answered.*

In the midst of this awful experience something wonderful happened to Hagar. She came face to face with God. "The angel of Jehovah or Yahweh" is thought by some to be a pre-incarnate appearance of The Word, who later came to earth as Jesus Christ. (This is only the 2nd mention of an angel in scripture.) Hagar must have been acquainted with God and His promises to Abraham. Surely one could not live with Abraham and Sarah for ten years and not come to know God. She may never have thought of him as other than "Abraham's God."

The messenger asked her two questions: Where have you come from? Where are you going? Hagar only had an answer for the first. This is often the case when a person is running away. All we know is that "back there" we face an intolerable situation. The way to determine if "running away" is the best solution is to come face to face with the Lord, as Hagar did. This messenger of God put Hagar back in her place as Sarah's maid.

Gen 16:9 ... "Go back to your mistress and submit to her."

The pregnancy had not changed Hagar's position in Abraham's household. Perhaps her lack of submission had been part of the problem. God made Hagar aware of the fact that there were more things at stake here than her relationship with Sarah. There was an unborn child to be considered, and even without an ultra-sound, God told Hagar she would have a son. *(Gen 16:10-12)* The people involved in this incident would have to face the responsibilities and consequences of their actions. Hagar was running away with no goal in mind. God told her to return and stay in her place. God recognizes human relationships and admonishes us to fulfill our obligations as wives, mothers, employees, citizens, taxpayers, etc., even when things do not turn out as we expected.

The Slow Upward Climb

While her emotional state was deep in the valley of despair, Hagar was seen by God himself. It was been very clear that she was nothing more than a slave, subject to the whim of her mistress. And yet the God of the universe had taken notice of her.

Gen 16:13 She gave this name to the LORD who spoke to her: "You are the God who sees me," for she said, "I have now seen the One who sees me."

Suddenly her existence took on a deeper meaning. Yes, she was still a slave, but her life had meaning and purpose. God knew the child she carried and had a future planned for him. We can say the same today, even when we are at the bottom of our own emotional roller coasters.

1 Pet 3:12 For the eyes of the Lord are on the righteous and his ears are attentive to their prayer, but the face of the Lord is against those who do evil."

This knowledge gave Hagar the strength to obey God's instructions and return to Sarah. We are not told how she behaved toward Sarah after this or how Sarah treated her. God's word came true and Hagar gave birth to a son whom Abraham named Ishmael, just as God had predicted. Sarah's plan to accept Hagar's child as her own obviously was not carried out. Undoubtedly Hagar was the one who "mothered" Ishmael. During the 13 years that passed before Isaac's birth was foretold, Ishmael was considered Abraham's heir. Abraham loved him, and Hagar must have been happy and more confident as each year passed that Ishmael would be Abraham's only son and heir.

Gen 17:18 And Abraham said to God, "If only Ishmael might live under your blessing!"

A Sudden Plunge

Life on a roller coaster is never calm for long. After Isaac was born and began to be given pre-eminence as the heir, Ishmael begin to resent him. The animosity shown by Ishmael toward Isaac was probably a result of the situation between Hagar and Sarah. This is not surprising. Children are always affected by the behavior of their parents. (Jacob and Esau; Jacob's sons) Sarah insisted that Hagar and Ishmael be driven out.

Gen 21:8-9 The child grew and was weaned, and on the day Isaac was weaned Abraham held a great feast. But Sarah saw that the son whom Hagar the Egyptian had borne to Abraham was mocking...and she said to Abraham, "Get rid of that slave woman and her son, for that slave woman's son will never share in the inheritance with my son Isaac."

The matter distressed Abraham greatly because it concerned his son. But God said to him, "Do not be so distressed about the boy and your maidservant. Listen to whatever Sarah tells you, because it is through Isaac that your offspring will be reckoned..."

By this time Hagar had lived in Abraham's household for almost 30 years. She must have been stunned at this turn of events. How could Abraham send them away now? But there she was, in the desert again. And this time she had a child to care for and protect. Could she do it alone? Although Abraham had sent her with provisions, they soon ran out. Once again God met Hagar in the desert.

> *Gen 21:17 God heard the boy crying, and the angel of God called to Hagar from heaven and said to her, "What is the matter, Hagar? Do not be afraid; God has heard the boy crying as he lies there.*

Getting Off the Ride!

When Hagar was sent away by Abraham, she was released from her position as servant to Sarah. She had a legitimate reason to leave, and God sustained her in the desert. As a single mother, she set about the business of seeing to the needs of her son. Just as Abraham carefully chose a wife for Isaac, Hagar went back to Egypt to select Ishmael's wife, but she did not go back to become a part of the Egyptian race, nor did she return to Abraham's household. She took God at his word, and watched as her son and grandsons grew into powerful nations. These nations interacted with Israel on a number of occasions. The Arab nations were not idolatrous, and they consider Abraham their father still today.

The name "Ishmael" means "God hears." The prophecy in Genesis 16 and its fulfillment in history are one of the proofs of the inspiration of the Bible.

Conclusion

> *Gen 2:24 For this reason a man will leave his father and mother and be united to his wife, and they will become one flesh.*

When God's plan for marriage is not followed, trouble results. In the case involving Abraham, Sarah, and Hagar, we see several problems manifested. There are others, as well.

- Discord between husband and wife.
- Rivalry instead of cooperation

- Hostility between the children
- Pride and Bitterness
- Divorce
- Emotional and Physical Abuse

This does not mean that when God's plan for the family breaks down, we are of no more use to God, but life may be more difficult. We may spend years on an emotional roller coaster, but when we are ready to get off of the ride, God will be waiting to give us the answers we need and the strength to sustain us.

God can use the fruit of a broken home, and his grace is sufficient to bring about successful lives. He will give us a second chance. Hagar, although an Egyptian slave, had a place in God's Plan. She showed strength as a single parent, raising Ishmael to be an independent, self-sufficient adult.

Hagar, the Egyptian

What difficult situations did Hagar have to face?	What good came about as result?

Genesis 12:16; 16:3-6; 16:7-13, 15; 21:8,17, 18, 20; 25:9, 12-13

What were the results when God's law for the family was broken? Genesis 2:24

THE ALLEGORY

HAGAR	SARAH
BONDWOMAN	FREE WOMAN
CHILD BORN OF THE FLESH	CHILD BORN OF THE PROMISE
MOUNT SINAI	PENTECOST
JERUSALEM ENSLAVED	JERUSALEM FREE
CHILDREN ARE SLAVES	CHILDREN ARE FREE
PERSECUTED	WAS PERSECUTED
CAST OUT	THE HEIR

For it is written that Abraham had two sons, one by the slave woman and the other by the free woman. His son by the slave woman was born in the ordinary way; but his son by the free woman was born as the result of a promise. These things may be taken figuratively, for the women represent two covenants. One covenant is from Mount Sinai and bears children who are to be slaves: This is Hagar. Now Hagar stands for Mount Sinai in Arabia and corresponds to the present city of Jerusalem, because she is in slavery with her children. But the Jerusalem that is above is free, and she is our mother. For it is written: "Be glad, O barren woman, who bears no children; break forth and cry aloud, you who have no labor pains; because more are the children of the desolate woman than of her who has a husband." Now you, brothers, like Isaac, are children of promise. At that time the son born in the ordinary way persecuted the son born by the power of the Spirit. It is the same now. But what does the Scripture say? "Get rid of the slave woman and her son, for the slave woman's son will never share in the inheritance with the free woman's son." Therefore, brothers, we are not children of the slave woman, but of the free woman.

Galatians 4:22-31

Jochebed, Jehovah is Her Glory

I was born a Hebrew in the land of Egypt about 1500 years before Christ.

My husband Amram and I were both from the tribe of Levi.

Although my ancestors had come to Egypt as honored guests, we were now slaves, oppressed by Pharaoh.

My faith in the promises of God remained strong in spite of Pharaoh's command to kill all male children born to the Hebrews.

I developed a plan to save the life of my son.

God honored my courage by returning my son to my care during his formative years.

Even though my son grew up in the palace of Pharaoh, he chose to suffer with the people of God.

All three of my children, Miriam, Aaron, and Moses, were used by God in the developing nation of Israel.

By faith, Moses, when he was born, was hidden for three months by his parents, because they saw he was a beautiful child; and they were not afraid of the king's edict.
Hebrews 11:23

Can I Save My Child From The Crocodiles?
Jochebed
Exodus 2

"These are the times that try men's souls." "It was the best of times; it was the worst of times." How would you describe the times in which we live? Precarious, affluent, hectic, uncertain, etc. Jochebed, the woman whose life we will study in this lesson, lived in a time described in the scriptures as "an iron-smelting furnace."

> *Deu 4:20 But as for you, the LORD took you and brought you out of the iron-smelting furnace, out of Egypt, to be the people of his inheritance, as you now are.*

The nation of Israel had gone from the "favored nation" status that they had enjoyed since their arrival in Egypt into a time of great oppression. They were slaves, completely at the mercy of Pharaoh. He spoke and their burdens were lightened or increased. Jochebed was just another slave, born in the obscurity of the hopeless, her future no different from her past, stretching into the years ahead with no hint of change. But for one brief moment she steps forward and takes action. It didn't change her life perceptibly, nor did her burdens become lighter. She lived and died a slave, bearing the burdens of the Egyptians. But others, in the distant future, would receive a tremendous blessing because of her. She acted for an ultimate reward—not immediate gratification.

Just the Facts

While the story of baby Moses is one of the most familiar in the Bible, how many people even know his mother's name? It was Jochebed. She was a daughter of Levi, but at the time of her birth that fact held little distinction. She was born to be a slave, no different from the rest of her tribe or nation. At the proper time she married and gave birth to a daughter and a son. Bringing new life into the world brought little hope for the future. It seemed Miriam and Aaron were destined to be slaves, just as their parents had been.

But this woman of Israel, whose name few people know or remember, had an ability born of faith. She could see far into the future—past this earthly life. God had made promises concerning Israel, and she believed God. So she raised her children as best she could, instilling within them the faith that she and her husband shared. When faced with the hideous decrees of a heathen king, she trusted God and acted in faith. Her life was not changed much as a result. Her youngest son was 80 years old at the time of the Exodus, so it is unlikely that she lived to wander in the wilderness. (If she did, she died there without entering the promised land.) More than likely she died as she lived—a slave in Egypt. But her actions had far reaching consequences that affect us even today.

Jochebed's Role as a Mother

All expectant mothers are concerned about the future of their children. This present time is as bad as any ever faced. In some countries, physical survival is the greatest concern. In America that may be surpassed by our concern for the spiritual well-being of our children. As Christians, the evil and immorality that is closing in from every direction should send us to our knees as we do spiritual battle for the souls of our children. We look to the church as a haven where we can trust the education and training of our children. But is it enough? Jochebed and her husband Amram were a part of God's chosen nation of Israel. Their children were God's people by virtue of birth. But something bad was happening to the children of Israel.

Jochebed's first child was a girl, Miriam. About seven years later she gave birth to a son, Aaron. Already the king of Egypt was looking at the nation of Israel with fear and superstition. In spite of his efforts to keep them in subjection by hard work and abuse, they seemed to be flourishing. He had ordered the midwives to kill baby boys even before they could draw their first breath, hoping the Israelites would assume that the infants were still-born and perhaps feel that they had been cursed by their God. The mid-wives refused to co-operate. They had learned to fear the Hebrew God and He rewarded them for this.

Jochebed's third pregnancy came at a time when Pharaoh had decreed that all Hebrew baby boys be thrown into the Nile River. This was no longer an undercover operation. How sad to think that the birth of a son would bring sorrow instead of rejoicing! Imagine waiting to hear, wondering a thousand times a day if your child was a boy or a girl.

As much as Jochebed might have dreaded it, her time came. **By faith,** when Moses was born, his parents saw that there was something different about him.

Acts 7:20 "At that time Moses was born, and he was no ordinary child (lovely in the sight of God). For three months he was cared for in his father's house.

Heb 11:23 By faith Moses' parents hid him for three months after he was born, because they saw he was no ordinary child, and they were not afraid of the king's edict.

Exo 2:2 and she became pregnant and gave birth to a son. When she saw that he was a fine child, she hid him for three months. NIV

Exo 2:2 And the woman conceived and bore a son; and when she saw that he was beautiful, she hid him for three months. NASB

Do you have a son or a grandson? What did you see about him when he was born? What would you have to know in order to act as they did, by faith? The knowledge that human life is precious would be enough for us to refuse to comply with the death order. Amram and Jochebed knew this and more. Obviously the promises that God had made to Abraham, Isaac, and Jacob had been passed down to them.

Gen 15:13, 14 Then the LORD said to him, "Know for certain that your descendants will be strangers in a country not their own, and they will be enslaved and mistreated four hundred years. But I will punish the nation they serve as slaves, and afterward they will come out with great possessions.

Although the Hebrews had been in Egypt for over 300 years now, they had not been assimilated into the culture. They were still a separate nation. Joseph's bones were still waiting for his people to carry them back to Canaan as God had promised.

Gen 50:25 And Joseph made the sons of Israel swear an oath and said, "God will surely come to your aid, and then you must carry my bones up from this place."

Obviously, Amram and Jochebed believed that God would keep his promises to his people. They were not going to be slaves forever. God had bigger plans for them. Can we have this same faith today? Do we look at the world and say, "It's hopeless. Our children are destined to be swallowed up by the current culture." Or can we look at God's promises and be confident that the power that raised Christ from the dead is sufficient to protect our children from the crocodiles that are snapping up those unwary souls all around us?

Going Once!

As a result of her faith, Jochebed took action. She knew that her role as a mother included protecting her child physically. For three months the family was able to hide the baby. Each day the danger became more imminent. Pharaoh's patrols were alert, listening for the cry of an illegal child. Perhaps the Hebrews who had complied with the edict resented the fact that Jochebed's baby was alive while their sons were not.

When hiding was no longer possible, Jochebed had another plan. God may have acted directly in guiding Jochebed, but not necessarily. She has had several months to think about this.

Acts 7:21 When he was placed outside,(exposed)Pharaoh's daughter took him and brought him up as her own son.

In a sense, the Kings's edict was obeyed, and yet the baby was protected. Not only was the "ark" lovingly prepared to protect the baby, it was placed in a certain place. Rather than just shoved out with a "God bless you, honey," it was carefully tended and watched over. No doubt ten year old Miriam had been painstakingly rehearsed as to what to do and say.

The plan worked and Jochebed's faith was rewarded. Her child was returned to her care during his formative years. She was paid to care for her own son by the daughter of the one who had ordered his death. God turns the wisdom of men into foolishness.

Going Twice!

When her son reached a certain age, Jochebed had to give him up again. Which would be harder? As difficult as it had been to set the baby adrift on the Nile River, it perhaps cost Jochebed even more to send her young son into a situation with the potential of changing him into a different person altogether. We do not know what contact, if any, she had with him after this point. She continued to be a slave, working the years away. Miriam and Aaron grew to adulthood. Still Israel was in slavery, with burdens growing heavier all the time. What was happening with Moses? What had been the point of her careful teaching and training?

Gone!

In recounting the history of Israel, Stephen describes Moses' education and training as he lived in the household of Pharaoh.

Acts 7:21, 22 ..."Pharaoh's daughter took him and brought him up as her own son. Moses was educated in all the wisdom of the Egyptians and was powerful in speech and action.

.

If Jochebed lived to see Moses take his stand with the people of God she must have felt rewarded. If she saw him rejected by his own people at the age of 40, she must have suffered with him. And then, Moses ran away. She must have wondered if that was the end of the story. At least he would not spend his life as a slave. At least he had not perished in the jaws of a crocodile. Jochebed had the satisfaction of knowing she had acted in faith and done what she could for her son.

Not My Child!

When others were giving in to the pressures of oppression, Jochebed stood firm. She had the courage when faced with the order to cast her son into the river to reply, "Not my son!"

Others may have said, "You have no choice." "It's the law." "Everyone is doing it." "You'll get caught and the results will be worse." "The alternative is too hard. You're crazy!" "You can only do so much." Perhaps Jochebed listened to their advice, but her faith caused her to look for alternatives and she found them.

As mothers today, we have to act with the same resolution, and say, "Not my child!" Others may say, "You have to send your children to public school (or put them in Day Care). You have no choice. Everyone else is doing it. The alternative is too hard. It is imperative that they get a quality education. How can you teach them the difficult subjects? They have to be able to compete when they get out into the world."

When that time comes, we too, must look for alternatives. It is not easy to follow through on the resolution,

"I will dedicate my child to the Lord".

The survival of their child in a hostile world was a top priority to Amram and Jochebed. It must be true with us. Whatever it takes, we must knock materialism out of first place and replace it with spiritual values. When you feel that both parents must work to provide necessities, examine your definition of "necessities." Is it: a car, or a second car? A house, or a big, fancy house? Suitable clothes, or stylish, designer clothes? If you come to the conclusion that you must work (and some must), this does not excuse you from your responsibilities as a mother. **Jochebed had to work,** but she still got the job done.

Amram and Jochebed did not just shield Moses from the unpleasantness around him, but they imparted faith to him. **There is a great difference.**

> *Heb 11:23-27 By faith Moses' parents hid him for three months after he was born, because they saw he was no ordinary child, and they were not afraid of the king's edict. **By faith Moses,** when he had grown up, refused to be known as the son of Pharaoh's daughter. He chose to be mistreated along with the people of God rather than to enjoy the pleasures of sin for a short time. He regarded disgrace for the sake of Christ as of greater value than the treasures of Egypt, because he was looking ahead to his reward. By faith he left Egypt, not fearing the king's anger; he persevered because he saw him who is invisible.*

Many in Israel had given up on the promises of God and joined the enemy in idol worship. (Go along to get along.) Moses chose to bear the reproach of Christ, rather than identify with the pleasures of sin. What did he know of Christ (Messiah)? Obviously enough to convince him that an eternal reward was more to be desired than temporary, earthly gratification.

Conclusion:

In spite of living in times described by God as an "iron smelting furnace" Jochebed and Amram were able to raise three children who were each chosen by God to do a great work for his people. Miriam was a prophetess. Aaron was the first high priest. Moses was the great law-giver and type of Christ. What made Amram and Jochebed successful? Can we follow their example and experience the same success?

- •They had **gifted** children. There is no greater gift a child can have than faithful parents. Every parent can give their children this gift.

- They had meaningful, personal faith. Jochebed and Amram have the distinction of being listed (though not by name) in the eleventh chapter of Hebrews.
- They did not conform to pressure. If they had, Moses would have drown or been eaten by a crocodile. If we dabble in the world, our children are likely to drown in it.
- They did not cease to plan. Faith and planning can co-exist. Do we plan for parenthood, to be teachers, to be servants of Christ?
- They were united as a family. Even the children were involved in the plan to save the baby. When Moses returned, Miriam and Aaron were ready to Exodus.
- When the time came, they let Moses go. Jochebed's faith allowed her to do her part and trust God for the rest. We eventually have to release our children to God. They will answer to Him.
- They had a goal beyond this life.

Heb 11:14-16 People who say such things show that they are looking for a country of their own. If they had been thinking of the country they had left, they would have had opportunity to return. Instead, they were longing for a better country—a heavenly one. Therefore God is not ashamed to be called their God, for he has prepared a city for them.

What are we doing to insure our success as parents?

"By faith, in spite of difficulties, by all that is in me, my child will grow up knowing and respecting God."

Jochebed, Mother of Moses
Why was she successful?

*

*

*

*

*

*

*By faith Moses, when he had grown up, refused to be known as the
son of Pharaoh's daughter. He chose to be mistreated along with
the people of God rather than to enjoy the pleasures of sin for a
short time. He regarded disgrace for the sake of Christ as of
greater value than the treasures of Egypt, because he was
looking ahead to his reward.
Hebrews 11:24-26*

Miriam

I was born a slave in the land of Egypt around the year 1500 B.C. My parents were Amram and Jochebed, from the tribe of Levi.

I had two younger brothers: Aaron and Moses.

As a young girl I was given the responsibility of watching over baby Moses as he was floating in the Nile River.

When Pharaoh's daughter found him, I brought our own mother to take care of Moses.

When I was about 90 years old, Moses returned to Egypt to lead God's people out of bondage.

I was privileged to participate in the first Passover, a foreshadowing of the coming Messiah.

After we passed through the Red Sea on dry land and Pharaoh and his army were destroyed, I led the women in singing a song of salvation.

I was one of the few women through whom God spoke to his people.

On the journey from Egypt to Canaan, I rebelled against the authority of my brother Moses.

God punished my rebellion by causing me to have leprosy.

When Aaron asked Moses to pray for me, he did not hesitate to do so, and God forgave me and healed my leprosy.

I was forced to remain outside the camp for 7 days, and all of Israel had to wait until I was allowed to return.

For forty years I wandered with Israel in the wilderness, but I was not allowed to enter the promised land.

I died shortly before my brothers and was buried outside the land of Canaan.

"Remember what the LORD your God did to Miriam on the way
as you came out of Egypt."
Deuteronomy 24:9

Will I Allow God To Define My Ministry?
Miriam
Ex. 2; Ex.15:20,21; Num. 12:1-15; Num. 20:1; 26:59;
Deu. 24:9; Micah 6:4

Miriam was a woman with a ministry. She was called by God to assist in leading the nation of Israel out of Egyptian bondage. This was a very important work that she was uniquely qualified to do. Very few women in scripture can claim the honor of being a prophetess, but Miriam is referred to by this title. She participated in the birth of a nation. Surely such a life of service would bring a feeling of satisfaction. And yet, at one point in her life, Miriam succumbed to a temptation that women still face in these times that try our souls. She refused to let God define her ministry.

Just the Facts

Miriam, perhaps best known as the sister of Moses, was ten or 12 years older than the famous law-giver. She was the daughter of Amram and Jochebed and had another famous brother, Aaron. Miriam was born into slavery, and spent the majority of her life serving the king of Egypt. When Israel was finally ready to leave bondage behind, Miriam was about 90 years old. What a glorious feeling it must have been to be free! Then, because of the collective unbelief of the nation, she spent the last 40 years of her life wandering in the wilderness.

As a child Miriam participated in the plan to save Moses from being killed. She was given the responsibility of watching over the baby and bringing about his reunion with his mother. After this incident, her life in Egypt is unknown to us. We don't know if she had any contact with Moses after he went to live with the Princess, a period of 40 years. After Moses left Egypt for Midian, her life was even more difficult. Miriam must have been more than ready to Exodus when the time finally came.

Exo 2:23 During that long period, the king of Egypt died. The Israelites groaned in their slavery and cried out, and their cry for help because of their slavery went up to God.

Tradition says that Miriam was married to Hur, a man from the tribe of Judah who seemed to hold a position of responsibility and honor in the young nation of Israel.

> *Exo 24:14 He said to the elders, "Wait here for us until we come back to you. Aaron and Hur are with you, and anyone involved in a dispute can go to them."*

If this tradition is true, her grandson was the artist chosen to do the intricate and beautiful work on the tabernacle.

> *Exo 31:2,4 "See, I have chosen Bezalel son of Uri, the son of Hur, of the tribe of Judah...to make artistic designs for work in gold, silver and bronze..."*

Miriam died near the end of the 40 years of wandering, without entering the promised land. Josephus indicates that Israel mourned for her 30 days as they did for her brother Aaron, who died shortly thereafter.

> *Num 20:1 In the first month the whole Israelite community arrived at the Desert of Zin, and they stayed at Kadesh. There Miriam died and was buried.*

Leader

Even as a child, Miriam showed distinct leadership characteristics. She was blessed with faithful parents who recognized in her the ability to accept responsibility and carry out instructions. She was dependable, and she was able to think and act quickly. Her parents must have known that. Children can be taught to obey the Lord.

> *Prov 20:11 Even a child is known by his actions, by whether his conduct is pure and right.*

They must learn unquestioning obedience to parents. It is all right to explain your instructions, but even if they don't understand, they must obey. A life could depend on it as it did in Miriam's case. Your child's soul may depend on it. It is absolutely essential that children learn to submit to their parents authority. From that point they learn submission to teachers, law enforcement, employers, etc. Submission to God's authority is the ultimate goal. This should be our objective in raising our children, not just gratifying a desire within ourselves to exert authority over someone else.

Miriam was not just "Moses' sister." As an adult, God chose her for a special work.

Micah 6:4. I brought you up out of Egypt and redeemed you from the land of slavery. I sent Moses to lead you, also Aaron and Miriam.

We see her in this leadership role as she led the women in singing after the Red Sea crossing. Singing is characteristic of the redeemed. We need to be reminded of our salvation. (I personally feel that this is one of the purposes of singing in the church.)

Exo 15:20-21 Then Miriam the prophetess, Aaron's sister, took a tambourine in her hand, and all the women followed her, with tambourines and dancing. Miriam sang to them: "Sing to the LORD, for he is highly exalted. The horse and its rider he has hurled into the sea."

Miriam performed a vital function at this point in the Exodus. Although the women of Israel may have been delighted to be free of Egyptian bondage, they would soon be facing trials of a different nature. Seeing God's spirit working through another woman must have been a great encouragement to them. Miriam, perhaps a wife and mother herself, could relate to their problems and understand their fears. This was a role that carried a great deal of importance in the time of transition from slavery to independent nation. What a great privilege Miriam had been given!

There is a great need in the church today for women like Miriam to take a role in leading other women in service to God. More and more women are occupying positions of responsibility in the world. It is vital that these same talents and abilities be put to use in the church. Wise, mature Christian women need to make themselves available as encouragers and teachers. We should not neglect this valuable resource.

Rebel

Being a leader-even one personally chosen by God-does not make one immune to sin. In Numbers 12:1-4, we see Miriam becoming dissatisfied with the ministry God had given to her. She fell into the sin of rebellion, which has its roots in envy. Throughout the scriptures we see the results of such envy. Cain killed Abel. Joseph's brothers sold him into slavery. Saul tried to kill David. The Jewish rulers crucified Christ. Miriam wanted to define her own ministry, rather than leaving it up to God.

Num 12:1-3   Miriam and Aaron began to talk against Moses because of his Cushite wife, for he had married a Cushite. "Has the LORD spoken only through Moses?" they asked. "Hasn't he also spoken through us?" And the Lord heard this. (Now Moses was a very humble man, more humble than anyone else on the face of the earth.)

What was the real reason for her rebellion? Was it really Moses' wife? Maybe Moses was paying more attention to his wife than to his sister.   In an effort to discredit someone, we often choose a controversial point in order to get people on our side. Perhaps this was the reason Miriam brought up the subject of race regarding Moses' wife.

Is it possible that Miriam was envious of Moses' position? He was, after all, her little brother. She had watched over him when he was a helpless infant at the mercy of the Nile River. She had seen him flee Egypt in fear after killing a man. Now he was looked up to by the whole nation of Israel. It seemed no one made a decision without consulting Moses first. Her own role had diminished since the Exodus. She did not get the recognition that Moses received. Whatever her motive might have been, God knew, and he does not tolerate rebellion against his appointed leaders.

Num 12:4,5   At once the LORD said to Moses, Aaron and Miriam, "Come out to the Tent of Meeting, all three of you." So the three of them came out.

Imagine the heart of Miriam as she stood before God. (Explain yourself, young lady!) She may have been defiant; maybe she wanted to have a chance to take this question up with God. The encounter must have been overwhelming. It seems to have left her speechless. God did all the talking, and the gravity of Miriam's sin is apparent from the punishment which God inflicted upon her.

Num 12:9,10   The anger of the LORD burned against them, and he left them. When the cloud lifted from above the Tent, there stood Miriam—leprous, like snow. Aaron turned toward her and saw that she had leprosy;

The effect of this disease was to classify one as "the living dead." Not only would Miriam's ministry not be elevated to that of Moses', but any interaction she might have had with the women of Israel would be over. She would be banished from the rest of the camp.

Wanderer

When Aaron saw what had happened to Miriam, he turned immediately to Moses. He obviously loved his sister, and realized the severity of her punishment. He confessed their sin, knowing the generosity of Moses' heart. God forgave Miriam in response to Moses' prayer, but the consequences of her sin remained.

> *Num 12:14 The LORD replied to Moses, "If her father had spit in her face, would she not have been in disgrace for seven days? Confine her outside the camp for seven days; after that she can be brought back."*

Her rebellion was made public, and the results of her sin were far reaching. Miriam's family was affected. Surely Moses was deeply hurt by the remarks that Miriam made about him. Aaron had fallen into sin because of her influence. The entire nation of Israel was unable to advance toward the promised land for seven days, waiting for Miriam's punishment to end. The women that she had influenced in a positive way, now saw her as one who was discontent and unwilling to serve God in her appointed role. Although God certainly forgave her, we hear no more about her ministry during the final years of her life. Instead she blends in with the multitude of people, wandering in the wilderness for 40 years, waiting to die.

Anytime we sin, it affects other people, but when we refuse to allow God to define our ministry the damage can be great. As parents, our disrespect for authority has a negative influence on our children. If we do not remain under God's authority, we cannot expect our children to accept our authority. The same is true in the church. Just as the nation of Israel was hindered by Miriam's sin, the kingdom of God cannot function properly when its citizens disregard God's divine design.

How Can I Avoid Miriam's Sin?

- Sincere gratitude for our blessings will keep us from envying the blessings of others.

> *Num 16:9 Isn't it enough for you that the God of Israel has separated you from the rest of the Israelite community and brought you near himself to do the work at the Lord's tabernacle and to stand before the community and minister to them?*

- We must quit comparing ourselves with others. Miriam was one of a select group of women to occupy the position of prophetess. At the beginning, her joy burst forth in grateful song. Apparently she became unsatisfied with what she saw as a "secondary" role.

Gal 6:4 Each one should test his own actions. Then he can take pride in himself, without comparing himself to somebody else,

- Recognition of God's appointed authority will keep us from rebellion. All authority belongs to God; He gives it to whom he will. How do we rebel against God? By rejecting his appointed leaders.

1 Sam 8:7 And the LORD told him: "Listen to all that the people are saying to you; it is not you they have rejected, but they have rejected me as their king.

- An understanding of our place in God's plan will keep us from taking authority that does not belong to us. Man's logic does not apply in the kingdom. First are last; last are first.

Mark 10:42-45 Jesus called them together and said, "You know that those who are regarded as rulers of the Gentiles lord it over them, and their high officials exercise authority over them. Not so with you. Instead, whoever wants to become great among you must be your servant, and whoever wants to be first must be slave of all. For even the Son of Man did not come to be served, but to serve, and to give his life as a ransom for many."

Mat 20:6 About the eleventh hour he went out and found still others standing around. He asked them, 'Why have you been standing here all day long doing nothing?'.....15,16 Don't I have the right to do what I want with my own money? Or are you envious because I am generous?' "So the last will be first, and the first will be last."

James 4:10 Humble yourselves before the Lord, and he will lift you up.

- Focusing on God and giving Him the glory will keep us from resenting the accomplishments (and authority) of others.

Eph 6:5-7 Slaves, obey your earthly masters with respect and fear, and with sincerity of heart, just as you would obey Christ. Obey them not only to win their favor when their eye is on you, but like slaves of Christ, doing the will of God from your heart. Serve wholeheartedly, as if you were serving the Lord, not men,

1 Pet 4:11 If anyone speaks, he should do it as one speaking the very words of God. If anyone serves, he should do it with the strength God provides, so that in all things God may be praised through Jesus Christ. To him be the glory and the power for ever and ever. Amen.

- If we love those who have authority over us, we will not envy. If we can't love them, we can "serve as if your were serving the Lord."

1 Cor 13:4 Love is patient, love is kind. It does not envy, it does not boast, it is not proud.

Conclusion

God has given each of us a ministry defined by our opportunities and abilities. If we will busy ourselves taking care of those things we know to be our responsibility, we will not have time to envy the ministry of others.

What a tragedy! Miriam slaved almost her whole life. She clung to her faith through hardship. Finally she was liberated, and was given the opportunity to participate in the birth of a nation. She was a prophetess and a recognized leader in Israel. Then, apparently because of envy, at the age of 90+ years, she fell into sin. She spent the last years of her life wandering in the wilderness, waiting to die.

Don't let this happen to you. Keep watch over your heart. Satan would have us early or late. **Remember Miriam.!**

Miriam and Aaron began to talk against Moses...and the Lord heard it....and said, "Come out to the Tent of Meeting, all three of you."
Numbers 12:1,2,4

How might each of these three spiritual leaders have felt as they stood before God? Why?

Miriam		
Aaron		
Moses		

Who are the leaders that God has appointed in our lives today?

How can we avoid falling into the sin of Miriam?

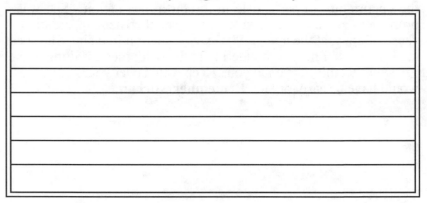

Rahab

I lived in the city of Jericho in the land of Canaan about 1400 years before Christ.

I was a prostitute living in my own house on the city wall.

When two Israelite men came to my house, I knew that they were spies for their commander, Joshua.

Everyone in our country had heard how the Israelites' God delivered the nation out of Egyptian bondage with mighty miracles.

Because of what I heard, I came to believe that the God of Israel was the only true God.

I hid the two spies and sent the king's men searching in the wrong direction.

I asked to be saved from destruction when the Israelite army attacked Jericho.

Joshua's spies promised that my family and I would be spared if we met certain conditions.

We met these conditions, were saved from destruction, and became part of the Israelite nation.

I married Salmon, a man from the tribe of Judah, and became the great-great-grandmother of David.

In Hebrews 11:31 my faith is given as an example to follow.

Matthew records my name in his account of the lineage of Christ.

By faith Rahab the prostitute did not perish along with those who were disobedient, after she had welcomed the spies in peace.
Hebrews 11:31

Will God Really Use and Bless the Sinner?
Rahab
Joshua 2, 6

There are certain people in our minds whose names are always followed by an identifying, descriptive word: Joan of Arc, Billy the Kid, Alice in Wonderland, Mary Magdalene, Simon the Sorcerer, Alexander the Great, John the Baptist, Jack the Ripper, Queen of Sheba, etc. Usually these are common names that might be confused with someone else. There are others, though, who have unique, distinctive names, and still have an identifying tag: Attila the Hun (How many Attilas do you know?) Rahab the Harlot. Even though she is probably the only "Rahab" any of us have ever heard of, her name is usually followed by an identifying term: the harlot (meaning "prostitute"). Actually, we know very little about her life as a prostitute. When we meet her in the book of Joshua, that phase of her life is over. From this point forward her life will be very different.

Rahab is one of only four women named in the lineage of Christ besides his mother Mary. All four were foreigners, not Israelites. Tamar, Judah's concubine; Rahab, the harlot; Ruth, the Moabitess, and Bathsheba, the Hittite Their lives are a confirmation to us that God does use and bless the sinner.

Just The Facts

The 40 years of wandering in the wilderness were over. Moses, Aaron, and Miriam, the leaders of the Exodus, were dead. Joshua the military commander had replaced Moses the lawgiver, and the mighty nation of Israel stood poised on the bank of the Jordan River, ready to enter and possess the land that God had given them. Jericho was the first city they would face. It was surrounded by massive walls—walls so big that houses had been built on top of them. Like most Canaanite cities, it was ruled by a king. Many of the citizens lived in outlying areas, and came into the city for protection when an enemy threatened. Joshua sent two men to assess the situation and bring a report back to him. When these two Israelites entered the city and inquired about lodging, they were directed to the house of Rahab, the harlot, which was located on top of the city wall. Their presence had not gone unnoticed. It would have been difficult **not** to notice the massive troop build-up just across the Jordan. All strangers were suspected of being spies. The king was notified, and soldiers were sent to the house of Rahab to bring the two in for questioning.

Rahab admitted that the men had been there, but insisted that they were gone now, and encouraged the king's men to pursue them. When the king's men left, she went to the spies where they were hidden beneath stalks of flax on the roof. She was not unaware of their purpose for being in Jericho. After talking to them about their God, Rahab let the spies down with a rope from her window. She advised them to hide until their pursuers returned, and then go back to Joshua. The spies gave her some conditions upon which her safety would depend. Rahab agreed with the conditions, and the men went on their way.

When God gave the word, the army of Israel marched on the city of Jericho. On the final day of the siege, Joshua's instructions to his men included this admonition:

Josh 6:17 The city and all that is in it are to be devoted (meaning to be sacrificed or completely destroyed) to the LORD. Only Rahab the prostitute and all who are with her in her house shall be spared, because she hid the spies we sent.

When the walls had fallen down and the city was being destroyed, Joshua sent the two spies to Rahab's house with instructions to bring her and all her family her possessions out of the city. They did this, and placed them outside the camp of Israel.

Josh 6:25 But Joshua spared Rahab the prostitute, with her family and all who belonged to her, because she hid the men Joshua had sent as spies to Jericho—and she lives among the Israelites to this day.

Faith

Rahab believed in the God of Israel, and because of her faith and in spite of her past, God could and did use her.

*Josh 2:9-11 and [Rahab] said to them, "**I know** that the LORD has given this land to you and that a great fear of you has fallen on us, so that all who live in this country are melting in fear because of you. We have heard how the LORD dried up the water of the Red Sea for you when you came out of Egypt...When we heard of it, our hearts melted and everyone's courage failed because of you, for the LORD your God is God in heaven above and on the earth below.*

She had not seen any of these things happen. More than likely she was a small child when the Red Sea parted. She had **heard**. Although she had been raised in a heathen nation and engaged in sinful practices, when faced with the evidence, she accepted the fact that she needed to be on God's side.

> *Rom 10:17 Consequently, faith comes from hearing the message, and the message is heard through the word of Christ.*

This places her in the category described by Christ when he told Thomas, *"Because you have seen me, you have believed; blessed are those who have not seen and yet have believed."* We also fit in this category. Did you see Jesus perform any miracles? Did you see the resurrected Lord? We believe because of what we have heard.

This willingness to believe says something about the condition of Rahab's heart.

> *Mat 13:23 But the one who received the seed that fell on good soil is the man who hears the word and understands it. He produces a crop, yielding a hundred, sixty or thirty times what was sown."*

Action

Not only did Rahab believe, her faith motivated her to act. She had already met one of the requirements of pleasing God. She had faith in His existence.

> *Heb 11:6 And without faith it is impossible to please God, because anyone who comes to him must believe that he exists...*

Now she must meet another, and she was willing to do so.

> *Heb 11:31 By faith the prostitute Rahab, because she welcomed the spies, was not killed with those who were disobedient.*

Apparently most of the Canaanites believed what they had heard about Israel's God, but they were not moved to obedience as Rahab was. Instead they chose to take their stand against God and the evidence that the Israelites were his chosen people. James describes this type of belief.

James 2:19-20 You believe that there is one God. Good! Even the demons believe that—and shudder. You foolish man, do you want evidence that faith without deeds is useless?

When she chose to be on God's side, Rahab found out that there were conditions that must be met if she and her family were to be saved. Her desire alone was not enough.

*Josh 2:17-19 And the men said to her, "We shall be free from this oath to you which you have made us swear, **unless**, when we come into the land, you tie this cord of scarlet thread in the window through which you let us down, and gather to yourself into the house your father and your mother and your brothers and all your father's household. "And it shall come about that anyone who goes out of the doors of your house into the street, his blood shall be on his own head, and we shall be free; but anyone who is with you in the house, his blood shall be on our head, if a hand is laid on him.*

She agreed to the conditions and set about carrying them out.

Josh 2:21 "Agreed," she replied. "Let it be as you say." So she sent them away and they departed. And she tied the scarlet cord in the window.

In the book of James Rahab is cited along with Abraham as an example of one whose faith was alive. The fact that she was a member of a heathen nation condemned to destruction by God did not exclude her from playing an important role in the plan of God. God was not concerned about Rahab's past. He wanted her "now." She had the courage to leave her past behind and place her faith in the God of Israel.

James 2:25,26 In the same way, was not even Rahab the prostitute considered righteous for what she did when she gave lodging to the spies and sent them off in a different direction? As the body without the spirit is dead, so faith without deeds is dead.

We often use the example of Rahab's living faith to emphasize the necessity of works in salvation. This is important when we consider our departure from the world and entrance into Christ. Faith alone is not enough. We must act. In the church this scripture has been frequently used to emphasize the necessity of baptism. However, James was writing to Christians, and the examples he used speak directly to us as we follow Christ in these trying times.

> *James 1:22 Do not merely listen to the word, and so deceive yourselves. Do what it says.*
> *James 2:15-16 Suppose a brother or sister is without clothes and daily food. If one of you says to him, "Go, I wish you well; keep warm and well fed," but does nothing about his physical needs, what good is it?*

Other New Testament writers also admonish us to act in response to our faith in Christ.

> *1 John 2:3-4 We know that we have come to know him if we obey his commands. The man who says, "I know him," but does not do what he commands is a liar, and the truth is not in him.*
> *Heb 13:16 And do not forget to do good and to share with others, for with such sacrifices God is pleased.*
> *1 Tim 6:8 But if we have food and clothing, we will be content with that.*

Reward

Because of her faith that motivated her to act, and her obedience to the instructions she was given, Rahab was rewarded. The physical part of her reward was immediate. She and all her family were spared from death when Jericho was destroyed. She found that God's word is true and that He keeps His promises.

> *Josh 6:25 But Joshua spared Rahab the prostitute, with her family and all who belonged to her, because she hid the men Joshua had sent as spies to Jericho—and she lives among the Israelites to this day.*

She married Salmon, a man from the tribe of Judah. Her son Boaz married Ruth, whose son Obed had a son named Jesse, who had eight sons. The youngest of these was David, Israel's greatest king and a type of Christ. Rahab's acceptance into the nation of Israel reminds of us Jesus' promise to his followers:

> *Luke 18:29-30 "I tell you the truth," Jesus said to them, "no one who has left home or wife or brothers or parents or children for the sake of the kingdom of God will fail to receive*

many times as much in this age and, in the age to come, eternal life."

Rahab also received a spiritual reward. She is listed with the heroes of faith in Hebrews 11, as one who gained a better resurrection. Her active faith motivates us to leave our sinful pasts behind and walk forward with Christ. Through her descendants the Messiah was born into the world, bringing life and immortality to light through the gospel.

Conclusion

How could God use a prostitute in his plan? According to one of the parables that Jesus spoke while he was on earth, just as he uses any other human—for we are all sinners—and more easily than some.

> *Mat 21:31 ... Jesus said to them, "Truly I say to you that the tax-gatherers and harlots will get into the kingdom of God before you.*

This was a difficult concept for the followers of Christ to understand. Surely the "righteousness of the scribes and Pharisees" would gain them first rights to the kingdom of God! Jesus illustrated plainly that a person's past was not a determining factor in obtaining God's grace. God wants our "now." Rahab's past was not what interested God. He cared about what she would do in the present.

> *The whole story recorded in the first few chapters of Joshua is a remarkable word picture of Christ and his church. The name Joshua is the same as Jesus. As Joshua sent out two men, so Jesus sent his disciples out 2 by 2. Just as the spies reported back to Joshua, Jesus disciples reported back to him. The admonition to Rahab to gather her family members into her house and keep them there during the destruction of the city is a parallel to Jesus' reference to the saved being in his church. The red cord in the window reminds us of the blood on the door post of Israelites' houses in Egypt that protected them from the death of the first born sons. That in turn is a picture of the blood of Christ that is applied to our hearts as a sign to God that we are protected. The instructions given by the spies were confirmed by Joshua in much the same way that Jesus told his apostles, "What you bind on earth will have already been bound in heaven." Rahab's reward of a new wealth of family in the nation of Israel matches the prom-*

ise that we will have, in this life, mothers and fathers and brothers and sisters and houses and land, etc., and in the world to come, eternal life.

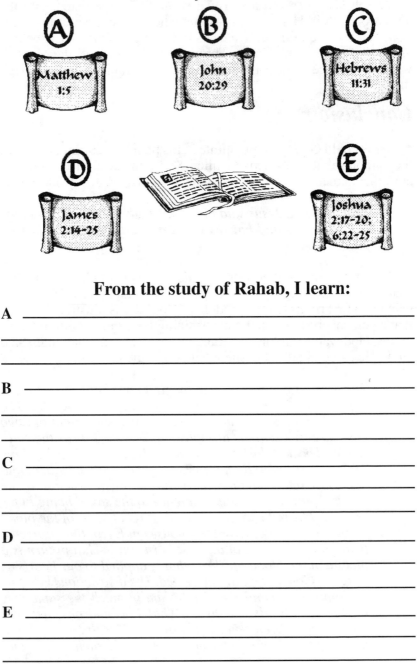

Ⓐ Matthew 1:5

Ⓑ John 20:29

Ⓒ Hebrews 11:31

Ⓓ James 2:14-25

Ⓔ Joshua 2:17-20; 6:22-25

From the study of Rahab, I learn:

A _____

_____

_____

B _____

_____

_____

C _____

_____

_____

D _____

_____

_____

E _____

_____

_____

ACROSS

3. I was a gospel writer who recorded the lineage of Christ.
6. I was an Amorite king destroyed by the Israelites.
7. I lived in a house built on a city wall.
8. I succeeded Moses as leader of Israel.
11. I was an Amorite king destroyed by the Israelites.
12. Our God delivered us from Egyptian bondage.
13. It is impossible to please God without this.
14. Faith without works is _____ .
16. Rahab married into this tribe of Israel.

DOWN

1. Joshua sent two of these into Jericho.
2. I was the great-great grand-father of David.
4. This New Testament book contains a chapter listing heroes of faith.
5. God promised this land to the descendants of Abraham.
8. This city was surrounded by thick walls.
9. Flax was dried here.
10. This New Testament book states that Rahab had a living faith.
15. I was Rahab's famous great-great grandson.

Deborah,
Judge of Israel

I lived in the period of Israel's history when "every one did what was right in his own eyes."

Since the death of Joshua, my people were constantly falling into idolatry, turning their backs on God.

When this happened, God allowed foreign kings to oppress us.

During my lifetime, Jabin, King of the Canaanites, was making life miserable for Israel.

My people had begun to cry to God for deliverance.

All Israel came to me for judgment as I sat under my palm tree.

God revealed to me His plan to free Israel from oppression.

I called Barak to lead an army of Israel against King Jabin and Sisera, the captain of his army.

He refused to go unless I went with him, and I agreed to go.

God fought for Israel and King Jabin of Canaan was defeated.

A woman named Jael killed the mighty Sisera as he fled from the Israelite army.

Barak and I sang a song praising God for the deliverance of His people Israel.

After this victory, Israel lived in peace for forty years.

"So may all your enemies perish, O Lord!
But may they who love you be like the sun
when it rises in its strength."
Judges 5:31

Can I Move Beyond My Present Level Of Service?
Deborah
Judges 4,5

Deborah is one of the most talented women we read about in the Bible. As wife, mother, prophetess, judge, poetess, singer, and leader in war, she demonstrates the power of one life dedicated to the Lord. She could certainly be described as a woman who filled a position that is uncharacteristic for a woman, and yet she remained within the will of God. How was she able to accomplish this? What was it in her life that allowed her to be the submissive woman that God wanted her to be and yet be involved in work that took her outside of her home and into an area usually dominated by men? By studying her life, we, too, will be able to maintain that crucial balance that allows us to use the gifts and talents that God has given us in a way that brings glory to His name.

Just The Facts

Times were hard in Israel. Jabin, king of the Canaanites, had taken over the land. The captain of his army was a great man by the name of Sisera who commanded 900 chariots of iron. The people of Israel were afraid to walk on the main roads of their own country, but had to use round-about routes. This miserable situation continued for 20 years. As in other times of distress, the Hebrews cried out to the God of their fathers. They had forsaken him for idols during the time of prosperity, but now they needed his help. Why did God continue to rescue these people who would not remain faithful? (Not to mention the fact that he loved them!) Remember that the nation of Israel was chosen by God to keep the knowledge of the one true God alive in the world. The Messiah would come into the world through this nation, when the time was right. And so God looked for a man as he had done before and would do many times in the future:

> *Ezek 22:30 "I looked for a man among them who would build up the wall and stand before me in the gap on behalf of the land so I would not have to destroy it,* —in the time of Ezekiel, God had to say,— *"but I found none."*

This time, however, God did find someone, but the "man" was a woman. He chose Deborah for this important role. Deborah was already a servant of God. She was a prophetess, and the sons of Israel came to her for judgment. At God's direction, she sent for a man named Barak and related a plan for defeating Sisera, the commander of the heathen army. Barak agreed to go, on the condition that Deborah go as well. Deborah agreed, but assured Barak that the glory of victory would not be his. God would sell Sisera into the hands of a woman. Barak summoned 10,000 troops from Zebulun and Naphtali to join him in battle. Those who were summoned answered the call and willingly followed Barak and Deborah.

When it came time for the battle, Deborah did not lead the army. She seems to have watched from Mt. Tabor. Barak, joined by many of the men of Israel, defeated Sisera and the Canaanites. As God intervened, the Canaanites fled, and even the great Sisera was finally slain by the woman Jael, as Deborah had prophesied. The song of victory recorded in Judges 5 is a beautiful example of Hebrew poetry. Following this great victory, Israel had peace for 40 years.

Available

Why did God choose Deborah to step into a role characteristically filled by men? First of all we notice that she was available and already serving God in her present role as a wife and mother. Although she was Israel's judge, it seems that she stayed home and Israel came to her. She was not a circuit rider. She had not left her home and family in order to be a judge. When God needed someone to step forward to lead Israel, he chose someone who had already shown her willingness to work for him. By taking care of her current responsibilities, Deborah was given the chance to step into an area of greater service.

How can we possibly measure up to Deborah? We cannot do it by sitting around wishing we could do something great and significant for the Lord. We can start out as Deborah did. We can be available. That means that we must be serving God in our present circumstances. We see this principle applied in Acts 6. The apostles had a primary role that must not be neglected, even for another good work. If you are a wife and mother, God does not want you to neglect those responsibilities in order to do anything else, even "church work." If you are a single woman, whether you are a widow, divorced, or never married, you must be serving God in that role. If it is your responsibility to provide food and shelter for your family, God expects you to do that.

> *1 Tim 5:8 If anyone does not provide for his relatives, and especially for his immediate family, he has denied the faith and is worse than an unbeliever.*

God does not give people new responsibilities until they have shown their willingness to fulfill the ones they already have.

> Mat 25:23 *"His master replied, 'Well done, good and faithful servant! You have been faithful with a few things; I will put you in charge of many things. Come and share your master's happiness!'*

Suitable

Not only was Deborah available, she was qualified for the work that was needed. She had the wisdom to deal with people and settle their disputes. She realized that Israel needed to turn back to God, and was willing to take an active role in seeing God's will accomplished. Deborah had a strong faith in God that she was able to communicate to others. She had the courage it took to face the enemy. When Barak needed her presence for moral support, she was not afraid to say, "I will surely go with you." Her courage spread to Barak and on to the rest of Israel.

When it was necessary, Deborah was not afraid to call people to accountability. She pronounced God's curse upon the people of Meroz when they failed to respond to the call to arms. She told Barak that he would not gain honor from the victory, and she gave credit to Jael for killing Sisera.

We need to work in an area to which we are suited, as Deborah was qualified for the work to which God called her.

> Rm 12:6 *We have different gifts, according to the grace given us. If a man's gift is prophesying, let him use it in proportion to his faith..*

> 1 Pet. 4:10 *Each one should use whatever gift he has received to serve others, faithfully administering God's grace in its various forms.*

Do you have the ability to teach? If so, teach. If not, look for another area in which you can serve.

> 1 Pet 4:11 *If anyone speaks, he should do it as one speaking the very words of God.*
> Rm. 12:7b *...if it is teaching, let him teach;*

Are you qualified to comfort the sick or bereaved? Then do that.

1 Pet 4:11b If anyone serves, he should do it with the strength God provides, so that in all things God may be praised through Jesus Christ.
Rom 12:7-8 If it is serving, let him serve; if it is contributing to the needs of others, let him give generously; if it is showing mercy, let him do it cheerfully...

Can you lead, or encourage those who are in leadership roles? Can you pray? Do it.

Rm 12:8 ...if it is encouraging, let him encourage; ...if it is leadership, let him govern diligently;

Where did Deborah get all of her qualifications? It's obvious, isn't it? She got them by exercising her abilities as a wife and mother, and then as a judge of Israel. Will the time ever come when you will be able to move on to a more significant work? In reality, what is available for you to do right now is the most significant work you could possibly be involved in. It is certain that if you neglect it, God will not call you to anything greater.

Agreeable

When God shows us an opportunity to take on a greater task we must be agreeable. We cannot use our present circumstances as an excuse **not** to do the work that God has called us to do. "I've married a wife, bought oxen, etc." When God revealed to Deborah his plan for defeating the Canaanites, she did not say, "I'm sorry, God. But I'm very busy just now with my family. I'm already doing this judging thing, and if I take time off to find Barak and talk him into this, the people might quit coming to me."

Not only did she talk to Barak as God had asked, but when Barak lacked the courage to take on the task , Deborah readily agreed to go with him for moral support. Women need to be ready to serve the Lord in all the ways that are available to them. Jesus encouraged Martha to distinguish between the inconsequential and that which is really of lasting importance.

Luke 10:41-42 "Martha, Martha," the Lord answered, "you are worried and upset about many things, but only one thing is needed. Mary has chosen what is better, and it will not be taken away from her."

Perhaps we feel unqualified to do anything more than we are already doing. If that is true, that situation can be remedied by studying, attending worship services and Bible study, or perhaps working with a more mature Christian. We cannot tell ourselves that we will serve the Lord "later" when circumstances are different or when we are more qualified. We must be busy taking care of the work that he has for us to do now. Deborah was available when God needed her.

Conclusion

During the time of the judges, Israel had fallen into spiritual decay. As a result of Deborah's leadership, Israel had rest for 40 years.

> Judg 5:31 "So may all your enemies perish, O LORD! But may they who love you be like the sun when it rises in its strength." Then the land had peace forty years.

There is evidence that the church today is in danger of spiritual decay as well. Israel had to take several steps to rid themselves of this situation and remain true to the Lord.

1. **They had to wake up, and the awakening began with their leaders.** *Judg 5:12 'Wake up, wake up, Deborah! Wake up, wake up, break out in song! Arise, O Barak! Take captive your captives, O son of Abinoam.'*
2. **They had to turn to God.** *Judg 4:3 Because he had nine hundred iron chariots and had cruelly oppressed the Israelites for twenty years, they cried to the LORD for help.*
3. **They had to offer themselves willingly, beginning with their leaders.** *Judg 5:2,7,18 "When the princes in Israel take the lead, when the people willingly offer themselves— praise the LORD! Village life in Israel ceased, ceased until I, Deborah, arose, arose a mother in Israel. The people of Zebulun risked their very lives; so did Naphtali on the heights of the field.*
4. **They had to have a knowledge of God's will so that they could defeat the enemy.** *Judg 4:6-7 She sent for Barak son of Abinoam from Kedesh in Naphtali and said to him, "The LORD, the God of Israel, commands you: 'Go, take with you ten thousand men of Naphtali and Zebulun and lead the way to Mount Tabor. I will lure Sisera, the commander of Jabin's army, with his chariots and his troops to the Kishon River and give him into your hands."*

5. **They had to be courageous.** *Judg 4:9 "Very well," Deborah said, "I will go with you. But because of the way you are going about this, the honor will not be yours, for the LORD will hand Sisera over to a woman." So Deborah went with Barak to Kedesh,*

6. **They had to teach their children, so that they would not find themselves in this situation again.** *Deu 6:6-9 These commandments that I give you today are to be upon your hearts. Impress them on your children. Talk about them when you sit at home and when you walk along the road, when you lie down and when you get up. Tie them as symbols on your hands and bind them on your foreheads. Write them on the doorframes of your houses and on your gates.*

These are things that we can help accomplish in the church to-day. Can one life make a difference in the church? In the nation? What about in your home? What will be the result in the church if women fulfill the primary role that God has given them? What if we have the courage to move on to the next step in our service to God? Deborah did. You can, too. Here are two questions we must ask ourselves: Will God be able to use me in a greater area of service than the one I'm presently occupying? What am I doing now to make myself available and qualified to take on that greater role?

Deborah

Why was God able to use Deborah in a role typically occupied by a man?
She was
She was
She was

What are your primary reponsibilities as a Christian woman? (Wife, mother, sister, daughter, friend, teacher, etc.)	

Why was Israel subject to spiritual decay?

1 Cor. 15:33	
Judges 17:6; 21:25	
Deut. 6:6,7	

What can we do to prevent the spiritual decay in the church?

Judges 5:12	
Judges 4:3	
Judges 5:2,7,18	
Judges 4:6,7	
Judges 4:9	
Judges 6:6-9	

Delilah

My name is Delilah. I was a Philistine, living in the valley of Sorek.

Samson loved me and lived with me.

The rulers of my people offered me money to find out the secret of Samson's great strength.

Three times he lied to me, and escaped when the Philistines tried to capture him.

Finally, because I "annoyed him to death" Samson told me that he was a Nazirite and that his hair had never been cut.

This time the Philistines captured him, gouged out his eyes, and made him grind grain in the prison.

As Samson's hair began to grow again, he was brought into the temple of our god to entertain us.

Asking his God for strength one last time, he pulled down the temple killing more Philistines in his death than he had in his life.

And I discovered more bitter than death the woman whose heart is snares and nets, whose hands are chains. One who is pleasing to God will escape from her, but the sinner will be captured by her.
Ecclesiastes 7:26

Will I Carelessly Cause Disaster?
Delilah
Judges 16:4-31

Samson is one of the most complex characters in the Old Testament. He is a paradox, having incredible physical strength and devastating moral weakness. The scripture specifically mentions four women who touched his life. The first was his mother who joined his father in asking God for wisdom to bring up their special child properly.

The second woman in Samon's life was a Philistine who "looked good" to him. Against his parents wishes, and to his pain and regret, he married her. The marriage ended in tragedy, but God used it to punish the enemies of Israel. A prostitute living in the city of Gaza was the third woman mentioned in connection with Samson. A visit to her gave the leaders of the Philistines an opportunity to trap the champion of Israel who had cost the lives of many of their men. Of course, Samson's great strength enabled him to pick up the gates of the city (including the gateposts!) and walk away unharmed.

The last woman in Samson's life was Delilah, and she is perhaps the most famous temptress of all time. Her very name is synonymous with treachery and deceit. Solomon must have had her in mind when he wrote many of the proverbs.

> *Prov 5:3-4 For the lips of an adulteress drip honey, and her speech is smoother than oil; but in the end she is bitter as gall, sharp as a double-edged sword.*
> *Prov 23:27 for a prostitute is a deep pit ...*
> *Prov 2:19 None who go to her return or attain the paths of life.*

Just the Facts

Delilah belonged to a nation of people that was constantly at war with Israel. At this period in history, the Philistines had the upper hand. Samson was designated by God to inflict punishment upon these enemies of his people. He willingly engaged in a relationship with this woman who was not only a Philistine and an idolater, but a prostitute as well. This was not his first experience with foreign women or even with a prostitute. His marriage to a Philistine had ended in disaster. *(Judges 15)* His visit to a harlot in Gaza left him exposed to his enemies and it was only with his God-given strength that he escaped. *(Judges 16)* After such experiences and against the advice of his godly parents, what could cause Samson to fall into this deadly trap? The scripture says:

> *Judg 16:4 ... he fell in love with a woman in the Valley of Sorek whose name was Delilah.*

It is unclear if Delilah initially had any feelings for Samson. If so, they were not very deep. Heathen cultures do not create love for fellowman, but the attitude "look out for number one." She quickly agreed to "sell him out." What were her motives? Apparently money played a big part in her decision.

> *Judg 16:5 The rulers of the Philistines went to her and said, "See if you can lure him into showing you the secret of his great strength and how we can overpower him so we may tie him up and subdue him. Each one of us will give you eleven hundred shekels of silver."*

> *1 Tim 6:10 For the love of money is a root of all kinds of evil. Some people, eager for money, have wandered from the faith and pierced themselves with many griefs.*

She may also have enjoyed the thought of dominating the "champion of the Israelites." More than likely Samson's weakness for her caused her to despise him. It did not take her long to discover that the source of his strength lay in the Nazarite vow he had followed since birth. When she had his long hair, the symbol of his vow, cut off, Samson was left without God's strength and the Philistines easily overcame him.

This once mighty man was now an object of ridicule, and his humiliation brought reproach upon the name of God. The Philistines brought him in to entertain at a feast to their idol god, not realizing that his hair had begun to grow long again. Samson, who had achieved many small victories over the Philistines in his life, called upon God to enable him to have one last victory. By causing the temple to collapse, Samson accomplished more for the Lord with his death than he had accomplished in his life. No doubt, the temptress Delilah met her own death as she celebrated her victory over Samson.

Delilah's destruction of this man of God was deliberate and calculated. She knew exactly what she was doing. As women who love the Lord, we would never intentionally cause the downfall of a godly man. But might we carelessly cause disaster? Sometimes we may act without realizing the consequences of those actions. Many times lives have been destroyed where intentions were only good. How can we be sure that we don't follow the path of Delilah? Let us look carefully at her life and learn from her.

Methods

What were the methods that Delilah used in her efforts to get what she wanted? First of all, she exploited Samson's love for her. He wanted to make her happy, and so he tried to pacify her without compromising his vow to God. Knowing that he loved her, Delilah was not afraid to keep pressing the issue. Eventually he gave in and told her "all his heart."

Next, Delilah perverted her God-given feminine traits and used them to manipulate Samson. Although he possessed great physical strength, Samson was morally weak. He exercised little control over his sexual passions, and Delilah knew this. Rather than helping him overcome this weakness, (as a righteous, God-fearing wife would have done) Delilah used it to humiliate and destroy him.

> *Eccl 7:26 I find more bitter than death the woman who is a snare, whose heart is a trap and whose hands are chains. The man who pleases God will escape her, but the sinner she will ensnare.*

Delilah used another weapon of Satan as well. She nagged and worried Samson until she finally got her way. Solomon compares this method to a continual dripping.

> *Prov 27:15 A quarrelsome wife is like a constant dripping on a rainy day;*

Delilah was an expert when it came to nagging. Every day she brought up the same issue, and every day Samson played into her hands. Instead of telling her firmly that the subject was off limits, he pretended to give in to the pressure. The answers he gave came closer and closer to the truth. Even when Delilah's Philistine friends used the information in an effort to trap him, Samson continued to subject himself to her tactics. Eventually he could take no more and told her the secret of his strength. It was as if he would have preferred to die rather than face another day of nagging.

> *Judges 16:16 And it came about when she pressed him daily with her words and urged him, that his soul was annoyed to death.*

It is difficult to understand how one could rejoice in the destruction of another person, especially one who loved them. Delilah's deceit resulted in the downfall of a man who was intended for spiritual leadership. Samson, once a symbol of God's strength, became an object of derision for the enemies of Israel. More than likely Delilah met her death on the same day that Samson met his. Ultimately, God used her to bring destruction on many of the Philistines. Those who stand in opposition to God's will, eventually end up bringing glory to his name.

What About Us?

How different Samson's life might have been if he had loved and married a righteous woman! If our husbands know that we love the Lord, they can safely give us their trust without wondering if we are leading them astray. Love is a precious gift and should not be accepted lightly or taken for granted. We should honor the love that is given to us, and not use it as a tool to get our own way.

God designed marriage to meet our sexual needs so that we would not be ruled by them as Samson was. If your marriage partner has a weakness, it is your duty, and should be your desire, to help him to conquer it. Delilah exploited Samson's weakness, using his desire for her to control him.

Even Christian women can be guilty of this. Some so-called Christian self-help books seem to teach women how to manipulate man into thinking he is in control when he is really just doing his wife's bidding. The special characteristics that God has given to women are designed to meet the needs of men. When they are misused, what was once beautiful becomes tawdry and disgusting.

Some women have a tendency to use Delilah's method of constant nagging and persistence to get their own way. Perhaps we have made up our minds that we know what is best and must badger our mates into compliance. Our desires can blind our eyes to the cost of victory: Loss of peace and harmony, the love and respect of husband, the confidence of our children, destroyed marriages, and even the spiritual death of ourselves and our families. In the face of such loss, the sweet taste of victory turns to ashes in the mouth.

Satan's Methods

Not only can we be guilty of Delilah's methods and carelessly cause the destruction of others. Satan can use those same methods to destroy us. The love we have for another person can put us in the position of wanting to give them whatever they want, even if it compromises our commitment to the Lord. We must keep our love for the LORD above everything else, and cultivate the kind of love that does what is best for the recipient.

Women are not immune to the power of sexual passion. Satan can exploit this natural inclination if we put ourselves in compromising positions as Samson did. Constantly being exposed to lifestyles that the world accepts can erode our will to resist temptation. It is very easy to rationalize unfaithfulness, divorce, promiscuity, etc., if our mind is saturated by the depiction of such things as justifiable, pleasurable, and necessary for us to be "happy." Young people who opt for "living together" over marriage are falling into Satan's trap. Without lifetime commitment, it is very difficult to have a relationship that can weather the occasional storm. It is time for the church and parents, teachers, etc. to take a firm stand on God's word. Not only **can** we be different from the world, we **must** be.

Satan can also use continual nagging to wear us down and make us give in to sins such as illicit sex, unethical business practices, cheating on tests or taxes or marriage. Even our children are experts at this method of getting what they want. We must not let them cause us to comprise our standards just to avoid their whining. They must be taught that this is a method of Satan and should be avoided.

Conclusion

We have looked at the lives of two women in the scripture who were members of heathen nations and prostitutes: Rahab and Delilah. When Rahab was exposed to Israel's God and saw his power and might, she became a believer with an active faith. She joined God's people was saved from the destruction of her people and her city. She was rewarded with acceptance into the nation of God and a place in the ancestry of Christ.

Being a foreigner and a harlot did not exclude Delilah from God's grace. She also came into contact with Israel's God. She saw first hand the strength of Samson, and had an opportunity to become a believer. Instead of being moved to faith, she employed all her wiles to destroy this man of God. She perished with the unbelievers.

As women of God, we are blessed with many wonderful characteristics. It takes a conscious act of will to use them in accordance with his word. Guard against using the methods of Delilah and carelessly causing disaster.

Delilah

What's wrong with this picture?

What did Delilah and Rahab have in common?
How were they different?

What were Delilah's motives? _____

_____

_____

_____

What were her methods? _____

_____

_____

Name some things that can be lost through constant persistence and determination to have your own way.

_____

_____

_____

Michal

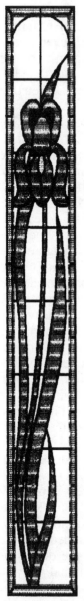

I am Michal, the younger daughter of Saul, the first King of Israel.

I fell in love with David when he played the harp for my father.

Because he had killed the giant Goliath, David had been promised the hand of my sister Merab in marriage.

When Saul became jealous of David, my sister was given to another man.

I was given to David instead, and only later did I learn that my father hoped that I would be the cause of David's death.

When Saul tried to kill my husband, I helped him to escape.

David went into exile in the wilderness, and I was given to another man.

Years passed before David became the king of all Israel and requested that I be returned to him.

By this time, he had married many other women, and I found myself the member of a large harem.

I became bitter, and as time passed, I grew to despise David.

When he put off his royal robes and danced before the ark of God, I met him with a sarcastic rebuke, criticizing him for mingling with the common people.

David made it plain to me that his devotion to the LORD would always take first place in his heart.

The life I had envisioned as wife of David, the giant killer, hero of Israel, was in striking contrast to reality.

Although David became Israel's greatest king, a man after God's own heart, I am last seen as a bitter woman, wife in name only, without even the comfort of children.

Her Name was Michal

(Introductory Reading by Emily Andrews Kile)

She was the younger daughter of Israel's first king. Her father, Saul, had taken royalty seriously, and elevated himself even above the rule of God. After all, he had been killing Israel's enemies by the thousands and the people were following his leading. But then her father had changed. The black moods came on him often. When that happened, it was dangerous to be around him.

It was during this time that Michal had first noticed David. He seemed to be the only one who could comfort Saul.  He played such soothing melodies on his harp. The words of his songs made the God of Israel seem so, well, so real and alive. To think that her father had promised Michal's older sister Merab to David in marriage! The very thought of Merab as David's wife made Michal's blood boil. It wasn't right! David should be given a chance to choose which of Saul's daughters he wished to marry. After all, hadn't he killed the giant Goliath with a simple slingshot when all the rest of Saul's army was paralyzed with fear? Michal was sure he would choose her if he were given the chance. Amazingly, when the time came for Merab and David to marry, Saul gave Merab to another man instead! Perhaps there was still a chance for Michal. She was in love with David. No doubt about that. Maybe if her father knew how much she loved David....

It happened. Saul offered Michal to David as wife. He even made it easy for David to accept. Since David had nothing to offer as a dowry, Saul asked only the death of one hundred Philistines. David had no trouble with that dowry. He even doubled the amount. The Philistines were no match for the giant killer. Saul had no choice but to allow the marriage to take place. Michal did not suspect that her father had ulterior motives for his actions. He planned for Michal to be a snare to David, a way to put him in his place. Too many people loved and admired David. Saul did not like playing second fiddle to a shepherd boy with a harp! With David as his son-in-law, Saul would be able to control him. He had actually hoped that the Philistines would kill David when he tried to obtain the quota for Michal's dowry. Nothing was turning out as Saul planned. It was obvious that the LORD was with David. Now he was son-in-law to the king, and Michal was not proving to be a snare to David at all. She actually loved him.

With David's increasing popularity among the people, Saul's dark rages came more often. David's harp playing no longer brought relief from the evil spirit that troubled him. Saul began to focus on David as the cause of his trouble. Finally he actually tried to kill David as he played the harp for him. Saul's son Jonathan had already told David that the king was trying to kill him. This time David took no chances. He fled from Saul's presence and went into hiding.

The first place Saul's men looked was David and Michal's house. Michal saw them watching the house, and urged David to escape before morning. She helped him out the window and then arranged a household idol and some goat's hair in the bed to look like David was sleeping there. When Saul's men came for David in the morning, Michal told them that David was sick and unable to leave his bed. Saul was not satisfied with the report they brought back and ordered them to bring David to him—on his bed if necessary— so that he could kill him.

The men discovered Michal's deception, and her father was angry with her for letting his enemy escape. Rather than defend David to her father, she claimed that David had threatened her life if she did not help him get away. It couldn't hurt to stay on her father's good side, at least until she saw how this whole episode turned out.

This was the beginning of a long separation between Michal and David. Saul denounced David as an outlaw and gave Michal in marriage to another man. David, although he had already been anointed by Samuel as Saul's successor, lived in the wilderness, struggling to survive. Somehow, David was not nearly as attractive to Michal in his role as "outlaw." As Paltiel's wife, she was treated like the princess she was. Still, she listened for news of David. Rumor had it that twice he had come close to killing her father, and had not taken advantage of the opportunity. It was also rumored that David had taken at least two other women as wives. Clearly, he had forgotten Michal. Well, she would not sit around and wait for him to send for her.

Meanwhile, Saul's kingdom was falling apart. His obsession with David was keeping him from focusing on the Philistines. Without the prophet Samuel to give him advice, he was unsure about what to do. Finally, the Philistines pressed their advantage, and Saul and his heir Jonathan were killed. David was immediately proclaimed king by the southern tribe of Judah, but Ishbosheth, Michal's brother, claimed the throne of his father. Civil war would last for 7 years, before David would be crowned king of all of Israel. When the remnants of Saul's men finally capitulated, David made one demand of them: "Give me my wife Michal, whom I betrothed to myself..." Without thought for the man who had been her loving husband, Michal was taken away and brought to David. Paltiel followed her all the way, weeping.

So, after a separation of many years, Michal and David were reunited, but things had changed. David was no longer the lowly shepherd boy, who had married above himself into the royal family. He had become a king in every way. All of Israel honored and respected him. He had been tested by time and adversity, and through it all, his dependence on God had grown.

His household had grown, also. Not only had he married Ahinoam and Abigail during his wilderness years, but he followed the tradition of the kings of surrounding nations. He had four other wives, and all six had given him sons. (He later took more wives who gave him 10 sons, as well as 10 concubines whose children are not named.) Even though Michal bore the distinction of being David's first wife, she became one of many. David was constantly occupied with an ongoing war with the Philistines. No doubt his other wives looked at Michal as the daughter of the man who had tried to kill David, and the sister of the man who fought against David's kingship. Being part of a harem was very different from being the wife of an adoring husband who treated Michal like the princess she was by birth.

Perhaps Michal never understood David's attachment to the LORD. It was as if David gave God all the credit for his victories over the Philistines. He was far too humble for a king. He treated his subjects as equals! What was the point in being king if you didn't set yourself apart and take advantage of your royal position? And now this obsession with the ark of the covenant. Things were going well enough with the precious ark where it was. But David seemed unwilling to let the matter rest, even after the first attempt to move it brought the death of a well-intentioned man who had merely reached out his hand to steady the ark on the cart.

The day came when the ark was on the final leg of its journey into the city of Jerusalem. Almost everyone was out in the streets wanting to be the first to catch a glimpse of the holy relic. Not Michal. She could see the length of the street from her window. It was a noisy and joyful procession. Many of the Israelites had joined in and were singing and playing musical instruments as they danced their way into Jerusalem. Michal could see it all from her window.

Suddenly she noticed the man dressed in the plain linen clothes of the Levites at the very beginning of the procession. Surely it could not be the king! And yet as the people drew closer to pass beneath her window, her eyes confirmed what she had suspected. It was David! Dressed in the ordinary clothes of servants, dancing and singing with the mob! How Michal despised him in that moment. Was it not enough that he had to personally lead the procession? Could he not have at least worn his Royal robes and conducted himself as the ruler of Israel! Well, she would certainly have something to say to him when he came home.

When the ark had been placed in the tent David had prepared for it, he gave all of his subjects gifts of food and sent them home. Then on this most joyful day of his reign, he returned to bless his own household. Michal met him at the door.

"How the king of Israel has distinguished himself today, disrobing in the sight of the slave girls of his servants as any vulgar fellow would!"

But David had something to say to Michal as well:

> *"It was before the LORD, who chose me rather than your father or anyone from his house when he appointed me ruler over the LORD's people Israel—I will celebrate before the LORD. I will become even more undignified than this, and I will be humiliated in my own eyes. But with the slave girls of whom you have spoken, I will be held in honor."*

This biting remark is the last recorded conversation between David and Michal. She stands, denounced and bitter, as the spotlight illuminating her in the history of God's people slowly dims and fades, leaving only this final footnote: *And Michal daughter of Saul had no children to the day of her death.*

Do I Become Bitter When Reality Falls Short of My Expectations?
Michal
1 Sam 18:20-24; 19:8-17; 2 Sam 6:14-23

A casual glance might lead us to believe that Michal was happy. She was the daughter of Israel's first king and married to Israel's greatest hero. Not only was her husband David a national hero, he was a deeply spiritual man who loved the Lord with all his heart. Such circumstances should produce happiness. But as we follow her life, it becomes apparent that her expectations made it impossible for her to be happy. Eventually her lack of spirituality was revealed by her concern for outward appearances. What caused Michal's attitude toward David to swing

From:

*1 Sam 18:20 Now Saul's daughter Michal **was in love with David**, and when they told Saul about it, he was pleased.*

To:

*2 Sam 6:16 As the ark of the LORD was entering the City of David, Michal daughter of Saul watched from a window. And when she saw King David leaping and dancing before the LORD, **she despised him** in her heart?*

Just the Facts

Even though Michal was the first wife of Israel's greatest king, her name is unfamiliar to many people. As the younger daughter of King Saul, she grew up in royal surroundings. When she married David, he was a soldier in her father's army. Although he had killed the giant Goliath, he came from a humble background. The majority of his life had been spent as a shepherd, a vocation that gave him ample time to develop a deep relationship with God.

Michal's father put his own desires above everything else. When he failed to fulfill his promise to give his daughter Merab to the man who killed Goliath, Michal was given to David instead. Saul hoped that Michal would be a snare to David. The marriage didn't last long. Saul's threats drove David into the wilderness, and Michal, at her father's whim, was given to another man.

After many years passed, King Saul died and David was eventually proclaimed king of all Israel. One of his first demands was the return of his wife, Michal. Over the anguished cries of her husband Palti, Michal once again became David's wife. Their relationship seems to have been merely a formal one. Michal wanted David to live up to her expectations of what a king should be. Her father had been her example, and he had rejected God. David was a man after God's own heart, and his manner of life reflected this. From the information given us in the scripture, we see Michal turn into a bitter, unfulfilled woman. Her last recorded remarks are sarcastic words of criticism toward her husband.

Expectations vs. Reality

Michal was raised as a princess. Perhaps she had a mental picture of what it would be like to be married to David the giant killer, hero of Israel. She would be the envy of all the women who had been singing David's praises. Since Merab had been promised to David first, her marriage might be considered a victory over her older sister. She expected her marriage to David to enhance her already elevated status. Instead David was reduced to the role of outlaw, and Saul gave her to a common man, with or without her consent. Life had taken an unexpected twist.

Has this happened to you? Perhaps you had health, education, marriage, and a rewarding career, only to find yourself suddenly physically handicapped, unable to work, and even abandoned by the man who had promised to "Love, honor, and cherish..." What are your options when faced with such a situation?

When David finally turned out to be the royal figure Michal had expected, she became the wife of a king. Now her dream-life would begin in earnest. But instead of sitting beside David on the queen's throne, Michal found herself a member of a large harem. David didn't even behave like a king. Most of the time you couldn't distinguish him from the coarse, rowdy men who were constantly surrounding him. Michal tried to tell him he was doing it all wrong—not taking advantage of his position and power. But he ignored her advice.

Have you been in Michal's situation? Perhaps you committed yourself to a man for life, expecting him to grow into the spiritual leader you envisioned as a husband. Years have passed, and he isn't measuring up to the standard you had set for him. You have given him advice more than once, and tried to change him, but it isn't working. The picture you had of married life has become distorted by reality. What will you do now?

Acceptance vs. Bitterness

Michal's problem was not unique. She was still judging David by Saul's standard. His position as God's anointed king was not able to penetrate her consciousness. Rather than seeing David as the "man after God's own heart," she clung to her own mental image of what he should have been.

Anytime we try to fit people into a mold we have designed ourselves, we are doomed to failure. Even if we are finally able to force them in there, they will not be the person we wanted them to be. We have to leave the molding to God. He is much better at it than we are.

Can we expect everyone and everything in our lives to live up to our preconceived scenario? Perhaps you have been told (as I have), "If you don't want to be disappointed, don't expect anything." Certainly, this is a true, if somewhat depressing, axiom.

> *Luke 6:34-35 And if you lend to those from whom you expect repayment, what credit is that to you? Even 'sinners' lend to 'sinners,' expecting to be repaid in full. But love your enemies, do good to them, and lend to them without expecting to get anything back. Then your reward will be great, and you will be sons of the Most High, because he is kind to the ungrateful and wicked.*

But don't we have a right to expect certain things? Certainly the scriptures teach us to look for the best in others, and to set goals for our lives. God expects certain things from his people, and we will be held accountable. Our expectations must be based on reality, and we must always be seeking God's will above our own. Only God is faithful and unchanging. We can always expect him to keep his promises. Yes, we can expect things from life and from other people, but if our expectations don't become reality, we must follow Paul's example:

> *"...I have learned to be content in whatever state I am." Phil. 4:11*

None of us want to end up like Michal, a bitter, disillusioned woman with no one to comfort her. What measures can we take now to avoid a similar fate?

Eph 4:31 Get rid of all bitterness, rage and anger, brawling and slander, along with every form of malice. Be kind and compassionate to one another, forgiving each other, just as in Christ God forgave you.

As we search the scripture for answers, one example looms larger than all the rest. How did Jesus keep from becoming bitter when he was rejected by the very people he had come to save? Since the beginning of time, God had been preparing the world for a Savior. When Jesus came to earth, he fulfilled every prophecy written concerning the Messiah. Surely he had the right to expect people to welcome him with open arms. When this did not happen, how did he react?

He could have become bitter and said, "These people don't deserve my help. They can just die in their sins, if that's the way they are going to behave." He could have said, "Well, I'm going to die for them anyway, since that's what I came to do. But they don't deserve it, and I'm going to be sure they know what failures they are." Jesus did not react in these ways. From his words on the cross we learn the secret to living without bitterness:

> *Luke 23:34 Jesus said, "Father, forgive them, for they do not know what they are doing."*

Conclusion

Does you husband fail to live up to you expectations? Forgive him. Did your children turn our differently than you expected? Forgive them. Has life dealt you an unexpectedly cruel blow? Accept it. Have you failed to accomplish your goals? Forgive yourself. By looking at the example Jesus set, we know that this is the right path to walk. None of us can ever hope to live up to God's perfect expectations for his people. Only Jesus did that.

> *Heb 10:8-10 First he said, "Sacrifices and offerings, burnt offerings and sin offerings you did not desire, nor were you pleased with them" (although the law required them to be made). Then he said, "Here I am, I have come to do your will." He sets aside the first to establish the second. And by that will, we have been made holy through the sacrifice of the body of Jesus Christ once for all.*

But, praise God, we can put Jesus on as a cloak, and when God looks at us, he will see his perfect son and accept us by grace.

How Did Michal's Attitude Change?

From: *Saul's daughter Michal was in love*
with David.   1 Sam. 18:20

To: *And when she saw King David leaping and dancing before*
the LORD, she despised him in her heart. 2 Sam. 6:16

What differences do you see in the backgrounds
of David and Michal?

David	Michal

Was Michal treated as "a pawn"? By her father? _____

_____

By David? _____

_____

Did Michal treat David as a piece of property? _____
What could Michal have done to change her position or her
attitude? _____

_____

Was she just a victim of circumstances? or did she make choices?

_____

How has Christ changed the standing of women? _____

_____

Abigail

I lived in the land of Israel during the time that King Saul was seeking to kill David.

David was living in the wilderness with many men who had joined his cause.

My husband, Nabal, was a wealthy man who was harsh and evil.

David's men protected my husband's flock and shepherds when they were in the fields.

At shearing time, Nabal prepared a feast for his laborers.

David sent some of his men to ask for provisions to compensate for the protection they had given his flocks.

Nabal treated the men contemptuously, indicating that David was a common criminal.

This report angered David, and he planned to kill Nabal and all of his household.

One of the servants told me what had happened, and I immediately prepared provisions for David and his men.

I hurried to meet David myself, and bowed to the ground before him.

I tactfully explained the situation, and reminded him of his position as God's anointed.

David listened to me, accepted the gift, and took his men back to camp.

When Nabal learned what had happened, his heart turned to stone and he died a few days later.

David sent for me, and I became his wife.

" Blessed be the Lord God of Israel, who sent you this day to meet me, and blessed be your discernment, and blessed be you, who have kept me this day from bloodshed, and from avenging myself by my own hand."
1 Samuel 25:32-33

When My Life Seems Unproductive, Will I Wait On The Lord?
Abigail
I Samuel 25:2-42

As women in the church today, we often find ourselves in circumstances with varying degrees of difficulty. Many of them are of our own choosing. Some are unavoidable. Some are a result of mistakes we made in the past. Some are the result of carefully considered decisions, but decisions that were made before we had dedicated our lives to serving Christ. There are some circumstances that we have the power to change. There are some that we cannot change. Some circumstances have little effect on how we live our lives. Others seem to be all-important, dominating everything we try to accomplish. Are there circumstances that are hindering you from being the person Christ wants you to be? What can we do about our circumstances? Indeed, should we attempt to do anything about them? When is it right to change things ourselves? When is it right to wait on God? I believe the answer lies in God's revealed will.

Just The Facts

Abigail was an Israelite living during the reign of King Saul. At this time in history, women had very few rights and were often treated little better than pieces of property. Abigail had the advantage of being born into a covenant relationship with God. The law of Moses protected women in many ways. It is most likely, however, that her marriage to Nabal had been arranged by her parents without her desire or even approval. The description given to us in scripture indicates the difficult situation in which she lived.

> *1 Sam 25:2-4 A certain man in Maon, who had property there at Carmel, was very wealthy. He had a thousand goats and three thousand sheep, which he was shearing in Carmel. His name was Nabal and his wife's name was Abigail. She was an intelligent and beautiful woman, but her husband, a Calebite, was surly and mean in his dealings.*

Abigail seems to have made the best of a bad situation. The descriptive words, "intelligent and beautiful" indicate that she had maintained a positive attitude. She was respected by the people with whom she had daily contact. She seems to have quietly served in the ways available to her. Seemingly, this was all life offered her. Even though she had great potential at her fingertips, she was hindered from using it because of the nature of her husband. But Abigail did not close her eyes to the opportunities around her. When Nabal made a very grave mistake that Abigail knew went against God's will, she did not hesitate to act.

David was a fugitive, hiding in the wilderness to avoid certain death at the hands of King Saul. Many men had joined his cause, realizing that he was destined to be the next king. This large band of "outlaws" lived off of the land, rendering services to various landowners by protecting their flocks from wild animals, as well as "human" scavengers. In return for this protection, there seems to have been an unwritten agreement of recompense. David and his men were allowed to partake of the various feasts that were held. Supplies were provided by those whom they had helped. This made it possible for them to survive in the wilderness.

David had performed such a service for Nabal, but when he asked for the expected payment, Nabal scoffed at David and his men, refusing to share anything at all with them. This enraged David and he vowed to kill every male that was in any way connected to the house of Nabal. Although Nabal was unmoved by David's threat (probably because of the alcohol level in his brain), his servants realized that a great tragedy was about to befall them.

Apparently because of her reputation for intelligence, Abigail is the one to whom the servants went with this urgent problem. She did not hesitate to take advantage of the resources available to her in order to avert this tragedy. A gift was prepared from Nabal's storehouse, and Abigail herself rode out to meet the coming destruction. The insight and discretion shown in the plea she makes to David is a lesson in tact and diplomacy. Without regard to the consequences she would face when Nabal discovered what she had done, Abigail took the action she believed necessary to protect her husband and his servants. Perhaps more importantly, she prevented the Lord's anointed king from committing an act of vengeance that would leave him with the blood of innocent people on his hands.

As a result of Abigail's quick and intelligent response to impending danger, God brought about a change in her life. Nabal was struck by the Lord and died. When David heard of his death, he remembered Abigail and what she had done for him. He sent for Abigail and asked her to become his wife.

Waiting on God

Abigail was a woman of great beauty and intelligence. Both of these circumstances are somewhat dependent on things beyond our control. Either one can be an asset or a hindrance. Abigail took what God had given her and turned it into a great asset. And yet, what could she do with these natural attributes from God? Her position as a woman and as the wife of a foolish, drunken man limited her opportunities to serve. She was also wealthy. But again, the wealth was controlled by her husband, and he was not inclined to follow God's instructions to use such wealth to bless others. In spite of circumstances that seem to us full of potential for service to God, Abigail's hands were tied. As the years of her life rolled by, she must have wondered what point there was to her life. What did God want her to do? Should she leave Nabal? She certainly was no good to anyone in her present circumstances.

What would you have done? Do you feel trapped in a situation that hinders you from using your talents and gifts for the Lord? Many times we feel that "if only I could change this one thing" then we would be able to do great things for the Lord.

How did Abigail respond to her seemingly unproductive life? It is true that Abigail was **not** responsible for many of her circumstances, but she **was** responsible for how she reacted to them. She chose to wait on the Lord. Her husband was probably chosen by her parents, but Abigail was faithful to him and took action to save his life. Apparently she spent her time doing the things she could do, and kept her eyes open for the chance to do more. This is not always an easy path to walk, but Abigail made sure that she always behaved in the way God would have wanted. She had no guilt on her conscience when she was finally given the opportunity to enter a new life.

Seizing the Day

Eventually a circumstance arose in Abigail's life that caused her to take action against her husband's wishes. Nabal's rash and ill-advised words, spoken while under the influence of alcohol, had endangered his life. Why did she choose to take action this time? She had remained passive through many situations, waiting for the Lord to change things if he deemed it wise to do so. Now she had the opportunity to let David and his men come and destroy her husband, freeing her from the trap that her life seemed to be. On the surface it may have seemed that this was the Lord's answer to her prayers.

But Abigail looked beyond her own desires and was able to discern what God's will was. In the destruction of her husband, many innocent people would also be killed. This was a great enough incentive in itself to convince Abigail to act, but there was something perhaps even more important involved. David, the man chosen by God to lead his people, was about to make a serious mistake. By taking vengeance in his own hands, he would drive a wedge between himself and the God that had always been his shepherd. David had been so conscientious to allow God to take care of his enemies, even to the point of sparing Saul's life when he had ample opportunity and justification (at least in the eyes of his men) to kill him. Now he was contemplating killing innocent people because a fool had refused to grant his request.

Abigail faced a decision much like the one faced by many of us in our own trying times. What would God have me do in this situation in my life? If I remain passive and let "nature take its course," the end result would seem to be the answer to my prayer. But God's will would be violated in the process, and I have the opportunity to prevent it. Recognizing the difference between "my will" and "God's will" is often very difficult. How can you be sure you aren't convincing yourself that something is God's will just because you want to do it so badly? How do we acquire the discernment needed to do this?

Eph 5:17 So then do not be foolish, but understand what the will of the Lord is.

Abigail knew God's law. Murder was prohibited by the law of Moses, and the shedding of innocent blood was a serious offence, carrying a stiff penalty. Abigail had a responsibility to prevent this from happening if she could. Knowing that David was the Lord's anointed gave her added incentive to prevent him from committing an act of vengeance that would be on his conscience and hinder his relationship to God. Clearly it was God's will that she use the assets within her reach to prevent this from happening. Her own desire was not a factor in her response to this situation.

Making the Decision

What does God expect from us today, passive waiting, or decisive action? Like Abigail, we have to understand what the will of the Lord is. In order to do this, we must have a knowledge of the mind of God as it is revealed in scripture. He has given us all we need to make wise decisions concerning our lives in his service.

2 Pet 1:3 His divine power has given us everything we need for life and godliness through our knowledge of him who called us by his own glory and goodness.

Are you concerned about finances, perhaps considering taking a job outside the home in order to raise your standard of living? If so, would it involve leaving your children in the care of someone who does not love the Lord as you do? Would a higher standard of living bring you closer to God or cause you to rely on him less?

Perhaps you feel, like Abigail, trapped in a marriage that hinders you from accomplishing your goals? Should you take action to extricate yourself from the situation or wait for God to bring about change if he sees fit, in the meantime looking for ways to serve within present circumstances? Remember, we must know what the will of the Lord is in order to make wise decisions. What does the Bible say about the sanctity of marriage? What does it say about putting God first and not compromising your commitment to his service? Will you leave your mate because marriage to him isn't what you expected it to be? Will you remain in a difficult marriage, but allow your heart to become bitter and vindictive? Or will you dedicate yourself to being the person God intends for you to be, even if you cannot see how your circumstances fit into his plan?

In addition to knowing what the scripture says about different situations, we must have a personal relationship with God through His son Jesus Christ, supported by daily prayer. We need to know that God loves us and wants the very best for our lives. That knowledge gives us the patience to wait on Him. We also need to know when to quit allowing circumstances to hinder us from serving God. Time here is so short compared to eternity. We must make decisions in harmony with God's will. If we are truly committed to serving him, he will provide the wisdom we need to make these decisions and the strength to remain faithful.

Isa 40:28-31 Do you not know? Have you not heard? The LORD is the everlasting God, the Creator of the ends of the earth. He will not grow tired or weary, and his understanding no one can fathom. He gives strength to the weary and increases the power of the weak. Even youths grow tired and weary, and young men stumble and fall; but those who hope in the LORD will renew their strength. They will soar on wings like eagles; they will run and not grow weary, they will walk and not be faint. Teach me Lord, to wait.

Taking Action

Once Abigail made the decision to act, she wasted no time in carrying out her plan. Notice the wisdom that she exhibits in her manner of accomplishing this imposing task.

- She showed great courage in riding out to meet David and his 400 angry men as they came on their mission of vengeance. *v. 20*
- She showed proper humility, using diplomacy in dealing with an angry, powerful person. *v. 23-31.*
- She accepts the blame that is rightfully her husband's. If she had disassociated herself from the problem, David might still have committed this sin. "I had nothing to do with this. It was that foolish husband of mine. It's all his fault." David might have replied, "That's great, honey. Now stand aside while I teach that foolish husband of yours a lesson." *v. 24*
- She cared about David's soul. She indicates that it is beneath David's dignity to deal with one such as Nabal. She recognized David as the Lord's anointed. She reminds David of his position with God, making reference to the sling. *vv. 25,26*
- She asks forgiveness and offers a gift. This was to satisfy David's men. They were angry and probably hungry. *vv. 27,28*
- She points to the future, helping David to realize what effect his actions would have later. (How we need to do this!) *vv. 29-31*
- David was restrained from sin and attributed Abigail with that accomplishment. She describes the guilt he would bear as a staggering burden. *vv. 32-35*
- She waited until the proper time to tell Nabal of his narrow escape. *vv. 36-37*

Receiving the Reward

Abigail put herself in a position to receive God's blessing by remaining within his will. God was responsible for Nabal's death, not Abigail or David. *v.38* This is in striking contrast with David's actions in dealing with Uriah. In order to get what he wanted, he compounded his sin of adultery by committing murder. This separated him from God until he repented. The consequences of his sin were far reaching and severe.

Abigail's attitude and actions caused David to recognize God's hand in these incidents, and also the value of a woman such as Abigail. *vv. 39-40* When he learns that Nabal is dead, David sends an emissary to Abigail, asking her to become his wife. Abigail does not lose her humility, but accepts the offer quickly as she recognizes God's leading. *vv. 41-42* As a result of her willingness to wait for God to change her circumstances, Abigail went from being the widow of a fool to the bride of a future king, God's anointed.

There are times when we know that God's will isn't being done. Then we **must** make a change in our circumstances. God will not necessarily cause drastic changes in your life here on this earth as he did in Abigail's. But later...

> *2 Tim 4:7 I have fought the good fight, I have finished the course, I have kept the faith; in the future there is laid up for me the crown of righteousness, which the Lord, the righteous Judge, will award to me on that day; and not only to me , but also to all who have loved His appearing.*

Abigail, Wife of a Fool

His name was Nabal and his wife's name was Abigail. She was an intelligent and beautiful woman, but her husband, a Calebite, was surly and mean in his dealings.
1 Sam. 25:3

Which of Abigail's circumstances do you consider negative?
Which do you consider positive?

Negative	Positive

(Are circumstances positive or negative in and of themselves? Romans 8:28)

How did each of these women deal with the " negative" circumstances in their lives?

Sarah Genesis 16:1-16	
Rebekah Genesis 27:1-46	
Ruth Ruth 1-4	
Abigail 1 Samuel 25	

89

Jeroboam's Wife

I lived in the land of Israel during the reign of Solomon, almost 1,000 years before the birth of Christ.

When Solomon died, the 10 Northern tribes revolted and chose Jeroboam to be their king.

The prophet Ahijah had told my husband that this would happen, promising him an enduring dynasty if he followed God.

Jeroboam did not heed his advice, but let the people into idolatry.

We had two sons: Nadab, who did evil in the sight of the Lord, and Abijah in whom the Lord found some good.

When Abijah became ill, my husband asked me to disguise myself and go ask Ahijah what would happen to our son.

Foolishly, I did as he asked me, but God had told Abijah that I was coming.

The prophet did not have good news for us.

Because Jeroboam had led Israel into sin, our family would be destroyed.

The prophet told me that my son would die as soon as I returned home.

This prediction came true, and all Israel mourned for Abijah.

Nadab became king after his father, but was soon assassinated.

As the prophet Ahijah had predicted, Abijah was the only one of the family to receive a proper burial.

The death of my son was tragic for me, but following my husband into idolatry was the greater tragedy by far.

"As for you, go back home. When you set foot in your city, the boy will die. All Israel will mourn for him and bury him. He is the only one belonging to Jeroboam who will be buried, because he is the only one in the house of Jeroboam in whom the Lord, the God of Israel, has found anything good.
1 Kings 14:12-13

Jeroboam's Wife
An Introductory Reading
by Emily Andrews Kile

Mrs. Jeroboam had problems with her children. Her older son Nadab was showing an inclination toward wickedness. He was sure to bring the wrath of God down upon his head if he didn't change his ways. But it was no use talking to him about it. Nadab would just scoff at the warnings of the prophet of God. After all, his father had defied God and gotten away with it. Jeroboam was still king of ten tribes of Israel, even though he had lured the people away from worshipping God in Jerusalem. The golden calves he had set up were a clear testimony of his disresgard for God. Nadab's mother worried about the future of her older son

Then there was the problem with Abijah. He was such a good boy. Even at his young age he seemed to realize that God was not to be trifled with. There was something about his heart that made it apparent that God cared for him in a special way. But Abijah was not physically strong. He was getting sicker and sicker. Jeroboam was very concerned about his welfare and was desperate to find out what was going to happen to him. He knew that there was only one way to know for sure. The prophet of God would have to be consulted. This would not be a simple task. Jeroboam would not want the people of Israel to know that he didn't trust his own prophets. That might undermine their confidence in him and the golden calves he claimed were their gods. And besides, why would the prophet Ahijah tell Jeroboam anything after the way he had rejected God? But they had to know the truth about their son's illness.

Perhaps Jeroboam's plan would work. She would disguise herself and go to the prophet. She would find out what she wanted to know without Ahijah realizing who was asking. After all, he was very old and was reported to be blind. Surely Ahijah would have encouraging news about her son. Abijah was such a good boy. All Israel loved him. He would make a fine king someday...

Foolish! So foolish! She should have known better. How can one expect to disguise themselves before the prophet of God? Physically he was blind, yes. But God spoke to him, and God sees all. She didn't even get inside the door before he addressed her as Jeroboam's wife. The news was bad beyond imagining. It just couldn't be true! What would she do now? Where could she go? Ahijah had told her that Abijah would die the minute she set foot in the house. She would stay away! She would never go home and then perhaps he would live. But how would she know? If he were dying, she wanted to be with him. It had all seemed so full of promise, this life as the royal family. Now she knew that it was all a sham. Jeroboam thought he could have it his way, that he could succeed without God's help. He would make Israel a great and powerful kingdom over which his sons and grandsons would one day reign. Well, all that was over. Ahijah had made it abundantly clear what the fate of Jeroboam would be. Destruction! Total destruction of the house of Jeroboam. His reputation was all that would be left, and what a fitting reminder of his life:

Jeroboam, the son of Nebat, who led Israel to sin.

Will God See Through My Disguises?
Jeroboam's Wife
I Kings 14

I have heard it said that we are many different people: The person we **think** we are, the person **other people** think we are, the person we **think** people think we are, and the person God knows we are. As you examine your life, do you find this to be true? When you enter the assembly to worship, do you put on your "confident Christian" face? Many people do. They know just what to say to convey the impression that they have their lives all together. How would that mask compare to the one they were wearing on Saturday night, or perhaps early Sunday morning as they struggled to get everyone to church on time? What mask do you wear when you approach the throne of God in prayer? Do you disguise your pride as humility? Do we praise him with our lips, when our hearts are really far from him? It is difficult for us to just "be ourselves." Our minds are constantly assessing what other people are thinking. We may be successful in disguising ourselves before the world, the church, our families, and even ourselves. But wearing a disguise before God is an exercise in futility. An incident in the Old Testament points this out in a very vivid way.

Just the Facts

Jeroboam was the man chosen by God to be king of the ten northern tribes of Israel when the kingdom divided after Solomon's death.

> *1 Ki 11:30-31 and Ahijah took hold of the new cloak he was wearing and tore it into twelve pieces. Then he said to Jeroboam, "Take ten pieces for yourself, for this is what the LORD, the God of Israel, says: 'See, I am going to tear the kingdom out of Solomon's hand and give you ten tribes.*

It may seem to us that the only role Jeroboam played was that of a spoiler. Since the Northern kingdom was eventually taken into captivity and never returned to the status of the Southern kingdom, Jeroboam's role was a temporary one, and limited in scope. But what God offered Jeroboam was much more than a temporary job. God promised him a dynasty equal to David's if he walked in the way of the Lord.

1 Ki 11:38 If you do whatever I command you and walk in my ways and do what is right in my eyes by keeping my statutes and commands, as David my servant did, I will be with you. I will build you a dynasty as enduring as the one I built for David and will give Israel to you.

But Jeroboam did not obey God; he felt he could accomplish all this without God's help. He set up idols in Israel to keep the people from going to Jerusalem to worship, fearing they would return to Rehoboam.

1 Ki 12:28 After seeking advice, the king made two golden calves. He said to the people, "It is too much for you to go up to Jerusalem. Here are your gods, O Israel, who brought you up out of Egypt."

When God sent a prophet to warn Jeroboam of the consequences of this act of rebellion against God *(1 Ki 13:1-6)*, Jeroboam tried to have the prophet silenced, but as he stretched out his hand to give the order, it withered and became useless. Recognizing God's power, Jeroboam asked the prophet to pray for him, and his hand was restored. The prophet promised Jeroboam a sign to prove that he spoke from God, and the sign came true. But...

1 Ki 13:33-34 Even after this, Jeroboam did not change his evil ways, but once more appointed priests for the high places from all sorts of people. Anyone who wanted to become a priest he consecrated for the high places. This was the sin of the house of Jeroboam that led to its downfall and to its destruction from the face of the earth.

When Jeroboam's wife is first mentioned in the scripture, she had followed Jeroboam in the path he had already chosen to walk. We know nothing of her life apart from him. She had two sons, Abijah and Nadab, both of whom could have caused their parents considerable concern—one because of physical illness and the other because of spiritual illness. The physical illness of Abijah is the circumstance that brings Jeroboam's wife to our attention. Her concern for her child creates a bond between Mrs. Jeroboam and all of us who are mothers and grandmothers today. Her story does not end happily, and she evokes our sympathy because of her suffering. But we can learn from her mistakes, and even if we are unable to alter the outcome of our children's lives (as she was unable to alter the fate of her child), we have a tremendous advantage over her: **We** can approach God without any disguises and find the help and comfort we need.

> *Heb 4:16 Let us then approach the throne of grace with confidence, so that we may receive mercy and find grace to help us in our time of need.*

The Choice

Perhaps Jeroboam was still a common laborer when he married. If so, becoming the wife of a king would have been a tremendous life change for Mrs. Jeroboam. The promise of a an enduring dynasty meant that her sons would have the opportunity for a wonderful future. When her husband decided to go against God's law, she had a decision to make. We don't know if this created a moral struggle for her or not, but she followed her husband into sin. Not all of Israel did. Everyone made a choice.

> *2 Chr 11:16 Those from every tribe of Israel who set their hearts on seeking the LORD, the God of Israel, followed the Levites to Jerusalem to offer sacrifices to the LORD, the God of their fathers.*

Like most mothers, Jeroboam's wife was concerned about her children. Her son Abijah became physically ill. It was doubtful that he would survive his illness. This created a very difficult situation for Jeroboam and his wife. There seems to be no doubt that they recognized the limitations of the "gods" that had been set up for Israel to worship. They had openly rebelled against God. The scripture indicates that Jeroboam deliberately "thrust God behind his back." *(1 Kings 14:9)* Now they needed help that only the true God could provide.

The Consequences

The Jeroboams had cast themselves in a certain role in the eyes of the people of Israel. In order to remain in control of the nation, Israel must be confident that Jeroboam trusted the golden calves as much as they did. This presented them with a dilemma. If they went to inquire of God's prophet as idolaters, they could not expect any help. If they repented and humbled themselves before God, they could not expect the Israelites to follow them in their hypocrisy any longer.

Jeroboam's solution to this problem may seem ludicrous to us, but upon closer examination we may find that we are not so different in our thinking.

> *1 Ki 14:2-3 and Jeroboam said to his wife, "Go, disguise yourself, so you won't be recognized as the wife of Jeroboam. Then go to Shiloh. Ahijah the prophet is there—the one who told me I would be king over this people. Take ten loaves of bread with you, some cakes and a jar of honey, and go to him. He will tell you what will happen to the boy."*

The plan had two parts. Go in disguise, and take a gift. Mrs. Jeroboam, probably desperate to find help for her son, went in disguise to a man, who though physically blind, had the ability to see into the future. Ahijah did not need physical sight to recognize her, because God told him ahead of time that she was coming.

> *1 Ki 14:5 But the LORD had told Ahijah, "Jeroboam's wife is coming to ask you about her son, for he is ill, and you are to give her such and such an answer. When she arrives, she will pretend to be someone else."*

If Jeroboam's wife had any hope of success with her disguise, it was very short-lived. Ahijah confronted her immediately. He showed no sympathy toward this woman who had followed her husband in rebellion against God. Jeroboam had said that Ahijah would tell them what would happen to their son. In this prediction, he was right. The king of Israel had closed his eyes to God, but God had not closed his eyes to Jeroboam's sin. The news was as bad as news could possibly be. God made it perfectly clear to Jeroboam's wife that they would pay for their folly. Not only would there be no enduring dynasty. The family would be completely wiped out.

> *1 Ki 14:10-11 " 'Because of this, I am going to bring disaster on the house of Jeroboam. I will cut off from Jeroboam every last male in Israel—slave or free. I will burn up the house of Jeroboam as one burns dung, until it is all gone. Dogs will eat those belonging to Jeroboam who die in the city, and the birds of the air will feed on those who die in the country. The LORD has spoken!'*

As devastating as this prophecy was, it didn't end there: Abijah, the son who was ill, would not recover. He would die when his mother returned home. He alone, of the family of Jeroboam, would be buried and mourned. God had found some good in him and would mercifully remove him from the scene before the rest of the household of Jeroboam met its terrible end. Mrs. Jeroboam must have wanted desperately to avert the consequences of her sin. How could she prevent Ahijah's prediction of her son's death from coming true? But in the end, she had nowhere to go but home.

> *1 Ki 14:17 Then Jeroboam's wife got up and left and went to Tirzah. As soon as she stepped over the threshold of the house, the boy died.*

Needless to say, God was true to his word.

> *1 Ki 15:29-30 As soon as he began to reign, he killed Jeroboam's whole family. He did not leave Jeroboam anyone that breathed, but destroyed them all, according to the word of the LORD given through his servant Ahijah the Shilonite—because of the sins Jeroboam had committed and had caused Israel to commit, and because he provoked the LORD, the God of Israel, to anger.*

The Masks We Wear

Jeroboam and his wife wanted to hide their true identity from God. They knew that they could not expect God to bless them in their sinful state. What about us? What masks do we wear in an effort to hide our true identity from God? Do we wear the disguise of illness, hoping to convince God that our failure to serve him doesn't come from our lack of commitment? Perhaps we wear the mask of poverty so that God won't see our greedy, grasping nature. Do we cover up our lack of evangelism with a cloak of feigned humility, insisting that we are not qualified to teach others? Could it be that we are like the Pharisees of Jesus' day, wearing a mask of spirituality, but inwardly harboring carnal hearts?

If we are disguising ourselves to God, we need to examine our motives. Do we want the reward without running the race? Are we uncommitted or impenitent? Perhaps our motives are more honorable. Maybe we are ashamed to admit that we are weak and in need of help. Are we foolish enough to think our heavenly father won't see the real us? Do we think he won't **like** the real us?

The failure of Jeroboam's wife to disguise herself before the prophet of God should encourage us to examine ourselves. If we ask, God will search our hearts, and show us who we really are. The results will not be pretty, for our own righteousness is in the sight of God, only filthy rags.

Isa 64:6 All of us have become like one who is unclean, and all our righteous acts are like filthy rags; we all shrivel up like a leaf, and like the wind our sins sweep us away.

This realization is the first step in recognizing our need for Christ. Then, after we put Christ on in baptism, we have the assurance that when God looks at our hearts, he sees his perfect, sinless son and not our blemishes. This knowledge makes it possible for us to approach God without the need for masks or disguises. Praise God for this freedom in Christ.

Conclusion

Jeroboam and his wife only turned to God in time of trouble. Are we guilty of neglecting our relationship with the Lord when things are going well, then coming to him in time of trouble, bearing gifts in the form of empty promises and resolutions? God says there will come a time when he will no longer hear us when we call on him.

Isa 1:15 When you spread out your hands in prayer, I will hide my eyes from you; even if you offer many prayers, I will not listen. Your hands are full of blood;

Jeroboam found this out. He failed to heed the warnings of God and was destroyed. Will we learn from Jeroboam and his wife the futility of disguising ourselves before God? To depend on God in times of trouble, but also in times of peace? The certainty of God's word? Perhaps when we are able to stand before God undisguised, we will be able to discard the masks that we wear as we interact with our brothers and sisters in Christ.

Rev 3:14-18 "To the angel of the church in Laodicea write: These are the words of the Amen, the faithful and true witness, the ruler of God's creation. I know your deeds, that you are neither cold nor hot. I wish you were either one or the other! So, because you are lukewarm—neither hot nor cold— I am about to spit you out of my mouth. You say, 'I am rich; I have acquired wealth and do not need a thing.' But you do not realize that you are wretched, pitiful, poor, blind and naked. I counsel you to buy from me gold refined in the fire, so you can become rich; and white clothes to wear, so you can cover your shameful nakedness; and salve to put on your eyes, so you can see.

The Wife of Jeroboam
1 Kings 14:1-20

...Do not go on passing judgment before the time,
but wait until the Lord comes who will both bring
to light the things hidden in the darkness and
disclose the motives of men's hearts...
1 Cor. 4:5

"Why do you pretend?"

What other individuals or groups of people in the scriptures wore disguises?

	Who?	*Why?*
Gen. 27		
1 Sam. 28		
Mt. 23: 27		
Mt. 26: 48-50		
Acts 5		
Mt. 7:15		

What disguises do people wear in the presence of God?

What is the greatest lesson you learned from Mrs. Jeroboam?

Esther, Queen of Persia

I was born to Jewish parents living in exile in the land of Persia during the reign of Ahaseurus.

My uncle Mordecai took care of me after my parents died.

I knew that my people were chosen by God to bring the Messiah into the world.

As a young woman, I was chosen from among many beautiful women to be Queen of Persia.

A wicked man named Haman was determined to have all of the Jews of Persia killed because Mordecai refused to bow to him.

Mordecai asked me to go to the king and intercede on behalf of my people.

Entering the king's presence without being summoned would mean death unless he extended the golden scepter. I had not been summoned for thirty days.

In spite of the danger, I went to the king and asked that my people be spared.

The king granted my request. The Jews were given permission to defend their lives.

Haman was executed, and Mordecai was promoted to a position of high honor.

Because of my willingness to risk my life to save God's people, Jews celebrate with the feast of Purim every year.

"Do not think that because you are in the king's house you alone of all the Jews will escape. For if you remain silent at this time, relief and deliverance for the Jews will arise from another place, but you and your father's family will perish. And who knows but that you have come to royal position for such a time as this?"
Esther 4:12-14

Can't God Do This Without Me?
Esther

Our first response to this question is, "Of course! God can do whatever he wants to do. If I help, fine. If not, he will find someone else." Certainly this is true in most instances. However, when it comes to the matter of our own salvation, the answer has to be no. There are just some things that God cannot do without our help. A young Jewish queen by the name of Esther found that out. When God's people were threatened with destruction and her guardian pointed out her responsibility to intervene on their behalf, Esther's response amounted to, "Can't God do this without me?" Mordecai's reply was:

> *Est 4:13-14 "Do not think that because you are in the king's house you alone of all the Jews will escape. For if you remain silent at this time, relief and deliverance for the Jews will arise from another place, but you and your father's family will perish. And who knows but that you have come to royal position for such a time as this?"*

Of course God could save his people without Esther's help. But Esther and her family would be lost. There was no guarantee that the king would listen to her, but even if he didn't, God could use another avenue to deliver the Jews. However, if Esther wanted to be delivered, **she** had to take action.

Just the Facts

The book of Esther is unique in many ways. Although it is the story of Jewish people, the name of God is not mentioned in the entire book. The characters in this highly suspenseful drama play an important role in the plan of God, but nowhere are they said to cry out to him for help. The Jews, who had been in captivity for 70 years, had been allowed by the rulers of Persia to return to Judea. Led by such men as Zerubbabel, Ezra, and Nehemiah, the former exiles had rebuilt much of their homeland and restored the temple of God in Jerusalem. But not all Jews returned to Judea. Some, like Esther's family, chose to remain in the land of their captivity. Perhaps the decision was based on financial reasons. They may have been successful in business, or risen to positions of prominence as

Daniel had some years earlier. Many of the Jews now living in Persia had been born there, never knowing any other home.

Even though they declined to join their brothers in the return to Jerusalem, they had not lost their identity as Jews, and they adhered to the standards of conduct passed down to them from the previous generation. Haman refers to the reputation that the Jews had acquired over the years, and apparently saw them as a threat to himself, and perhaps the kingdom as a whole.

> *Est 3:8 Then Haman said to King Xerxes, "There is a certain people dispersed and scattered among the peoples in all the provinces of your kingdom whose customs are different from those of all other people and who do not obey the king's laws; it is not in the king's best interest to tolerate them.*

The special significance the Jews had in the plan of God must have been known to Mordecai. He was confident that God would deliver them from those who wanted their destruction. Their survival in captivity and success in returning to their homeland had given the Jews a reputation that commanded respect.

> *Est 6:13 ...His advisers and his wife Zeresh said to him, "Since Mordecai, before whom your downfall has started, is of Jewish origin, you cannot stand against him—you will surely come to ruin!"*

The book of Esther portrays God's care and protection for these people who were struggling to survive and maintain their distinctiveness in a land of idolaters. In particular it focuses on one Jewish woman who finds herself in a position to influence the destiny of an entire nation.

Trying Times

What can we learn from this beautiful Jewish woman? Her life certainly does not parallel mine. The Bible does not tell us if she ever became a mother. She was not really a wife in the traditional sense, but was the top member of a large harem, seeing her husband only occasionally and at his request. An orphan, raised by her uncle Mordecai, her early life was probably typical of the other Jewish people who lived in the land of Persia. She was most likely still a teenager when her life changed drastically. She was chosen to compete for the position of queen that had been left open when Xerxes had deposed Vashti some four years earlier. Her lifetime of training as a daughter of Israel gave her an attitude of graciousness and sub-mission that caused her to find favor with all who met her, including the king.

When she was chosen to be queen, Esther was separated from her own culture and even her family. She lived in the isolation of a harem, seldom coming in contact with anyone outside the palace walls. Esther was not absorbed into this new existence completely. Appar-ently, no one even knew her well enough to know that she was a Jew. Her early training continued to influence her behavior, however. She followed Mordecai's advice, even when doing so threatened her very life.

Perhaps you feel as Esther must have felt every time you go to work or to school. As Christians, we don't really fit into the culture of the world. Our ways may seem strange to those around us. In this sense, we can see many things in our lives that do parallel the life of Esther. We each have our own area of influence within the world. We are faced with challenges and opportunities just as Esther was. And, like Esther, we may need someone to point them out to us, and encourage us to take appropriate action.

The Threat of Destruction

During Esther's time as queen, God's people were being threat-ened with annihilation. Satan, working through the wicked Haman, was behind this plot. His agent of choice was the government. First of all, he intended to use his governmental position and his friend-ship with the king to gain a personal favor. What he wanted to ac-complish was the destruction of the Jews. He also planned to use his own financial resources to ensure that his wishes would accomplished. By convincing Xerxes that the Jews were a threat to the kingdom and emphasizing the fact that they were "different," Haman gained the necessary authorization to carry out his plan.

> *Est 3:8,9 Then Haman said to King Xerxes, "There is a cer-tain people dispersed and scattered among the peoples in all the provinces of your kingdom whose customs are different from those of all other people and who do not obey the king's laws; it is not in the king's best interest to tolerate them. If it pleases the king, let a decree be issued to destroy them, and I will put ten thousand talents of silver into the royal treasury for the men who carry out this business."*

God's people in our country today are being threatened with an-nihilation. Satan is behind this plot, and typically he is using the government as an agent to carry out his plan. Other agents of choice are the entertainment industry, false teachers of religion, drugs, etc. Christians are being characterized as a threat to First Amendment rights by those in governmental positions. The typical media presentation shows those who profess Christianity as being unbalanced, hypocritical, or as objects of ridicule. Satan has access to unlimited wealth, and he is willing to use it all to accomplish the destruction of those follow Jesus.

The Jews in the kingdom of Persia were aware that their existence was being threatened. It caused them great concern and they went into mourning. Normal routines were interrupted, and the people dressed in sackcloth and put ashes on their heads. There seemed to be no way out of this dilemma. They were not citizens of this country—only sojourners—and Xerxes was the most powerful ruler in the world.

Christians today are also aware of the threats of Satan. Throughout the country there is a rising concern over the decline of morality. Parents are voicing their alarm, warnings are being issued from pulpits, and political candidates are decrying the direction the government seems to be heading. In the face of opposition from the wealthy entertainment industry and powerful government agencies, the future of the Christian community may seem in doubt. Just as in the time of Esther, many see no way of escape.

Obstacles or Opportunities?

Looking back at the Biblical story, it is obvious to us that Esther was in the perfect position to intervene on behalf of her people. After all, she was queen and surely had the ear of the king. Esther seemed totally unaware of the possibilities her situation offered, but Mordecai had not overlooked this avenue of deliverance for the Jews. He was quick to point out this opportunity and ask for her help.

> *Est 4:8 He also gave him a copy of the text of the edict for their annihilation, which had been published in Susa, to show to Esther and explain it to her, and he told him to urge her to go into the king's presence to beg for mercy and plead with him for her people.*

Where Mordecai saw opportunity, Esther saw obstacles. No one in the king's household knew that she was a Jew. If she revealed her nationality in an effort to save her people, she would put herself in jeopardy, and for what? She had no power of her own, and the king had not sent for her in over a month. It would be breaking the law to go before Xerxes without being summoned. This edict that had been issued ordering the destruction of the Jews could not be rescinded, anyway. What could she possibly accomplish by doing what Mordecai asked?

> *Est 4:10,11 Then she instructed him to say to Mordecai..."*
> *for any man or woman who approaches the king in the inner*
> *court without being summoned the king has but one law: that*
> *he be put to death. The only exception to this is for the king to*
> *extend the gold scepter to him and spare his life. But thirty*
> *days have passed since I was called to go to the king."*

In essence, Esther was saying, "Can't God do this without me?" Mordecai's answer showed insight into human nature, as well as a knowledge of the plan of God. He knew that the Jews were a nation designated to keep the knowledge of the true God alive and eventually bring the Messiah into the world. He could say with confidence:

> *Est 4:14 "For if you remain silent at this time, relief and*
> *deliverance for the Jews will arise from another place..."*

Mordecai also knew human nature well enough to know how Esther and her father's family would be treated by the rest of the Jews if she failed to make an effort to help them. Perhaps she would be looked upon as a traitor who denied her nationality in order to save herself. If so, her life would not be worth living.

> *Est 4:14 "...but you and your father's family will perish. "*

Esther's Response—And Ours!

Esther had to face Mordecai's challenge. As she looked back on the chain of events that had brought her to her present prominence, the uniqueness of her position must have been obvious. It was certainly an unusual situation in which to find a young Jewish girl living in Persia. Perhaps Mordecai was right:

> *Est 4:14 "... And who knows but that you have come to royal*
> *position for such a time as this?"*

Esther's response to Mordecai's challenge is familiar to us. It was not an easy decision to make, but for member of the Jewish race there was only one decision. She did everything she knew to do in order to ensure her success, and then she took action.

Est 4:16-17   "Go, gather together all the Jews who are in Susa, and fast for me. Do not eat or drink for three days, night or day. I and my maids will fast as you do. When this is done, I will go to the king, even though it is against the law. And if I perish, I perish."

Someone is in a position to do something to stem the tide of destruction that threatens to sweep over God's people today. Perhaps it is you. Our time is no different from any other time in history. God is looking for someone to "stand in the gap."

Ezek 22:30   "I looked for a man among them who would build up the wall and stand before me in the gap on behalf of the land so I would not have to destroy it, but I found none."

Do we, like Esther, see obstacles rather than opportunities? Do we plead helplessness in the face of the world's resources? After all, we are just one person. How could one person hope to make a difference? Nobody cares what our opinions are. Getting involved in the social issues of the day might endanger our relationships in the work force. We could be breaking the law. Surely God wouldn't want us to do that. Besides, can't God do this without us?

One Step At A Time

Mordecai's answer to Esther is applicable to us as well. Of course, God can do this without our help. But what will that do to us? If we stand on the sidelines and refuse to get involved, our hearts will be affected. We will be ashamed of our fear, and our courage will diminish even more. How will we be able to face God in prayer? And what of our families and others within our realm of influence? Our apathy will be seen as tolerance, and our ability to lead others to Christ will be lost. The end of this course of action will be our own destruction.

John 12:25   The man who loves his life will lose it, while the man who hates his life in this world will keep it for eternal life.

As we follow the unfolding drama, it is interesting to note that this first step of faith gave Esther the courage to take the next step. Her willingness to risk her own life made it possible for the Jews of Persia to defend theirs. Their mourning turned into joy and many other people wanted to join their nation.

Est 8:17 In every province and in every city, wherever the edict of the king went, there was joy and gladness among the Jews, with feasting and celebrating. And many people of other nationalities became Jews because fear of the Jews had seized them.

Esther then had the courage to ask the king to destroy all those who had been a part of Haman's wicked plan. When the day planned for destruction arrived, the Jews defended themselves and won a great victory over the enemy.

Est 9:2 The Jews assembled in their cities in all the provinces of King Xerxes to attack those seeking their destruction. No one could stand against them, because the people of all the other nationalities were afraid of them.

Although Xerxes was not particularly interested in the fate of the Jews, because of Esther he gave Mordecai great power in the land and Mordecai was able to help his countrymen in many ways.

Est 10:3 Mordecai the Jew was second in rank to King Xerxes, preeminent among the Jews, and held in high esteem by his many fellow Jews, because he worked for the good of his people and spoke up for the welfare of all the Jews.

Conclusion

Just as Esther's first courageous step led to many victories, so our willingness to take the risk of standing for the truth will lead us to victory. Our courage will grow and our example will give others courage to act. The result will be beyond what we can understand or imagine. This kind of action will cause unbelievers to turn to God. Even those who don't really care about the survival of Christians will contribute to the battle, just to be on the "popular" or winning side. We do not know what God has in store for our country in the years to come. We do know that it is our responsibility to say with the apostles of Christ:

Acts 5:29   "We must obey God rather than men!"

"For Such A Time As This"

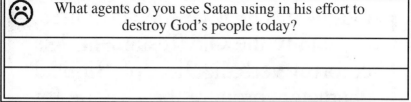

Why am I here at "such a time as this"? Phil. 2:15

What agents do you see Satan using in his effort to destroy God's people today?

What signs do you see that Christians are waking up to the threat of destruction in our country today?

Since few are in a position to influence national policy from the top, what can you do personally to hinder Satan's work in our country?

What does Acts 5:29 mean to you?

I would like to dedicate this book to my father, R. L. Andrews. He taught me to love the scriptures, especially the Old Testament. His colorful verbalization of Biblical characters brought them to life for me, and I appreciate the opportunity to share these women's stories with others.